Journey Through the
BIBLE

The late **Dr. Van Bogard Dunn,** writer of this study resource, was Professor Emeritus and Dean Emeritus at the Methodist Theological School in Ohio. He was a graduate of Murray State University and Duke Divinity School. In his long career as a professor and student of the New Testament, Dr. Dunn shared his knowledge with the general church, writing for both Church School Publications and Discipleship Resources. "Bogie," as students lovingly called him, was married to the former Geraldine Hurt, Bogie Dunn died while preaching in December 1994.

JOURNEY THROUGH THE BIBLE. An official resource for The United Methodist Church prepared by the General Board of Discipleship through the division of Church School Publications and published by Cokesbury, a division of The United Methodist Publishing House, 201 Eighth Avenue, South, P. O. Box 801, Nashville, Tennessee 37202. Printed in the United States of America. Copyright © 1994 by Cokesbury. All rights reserved.

Scripture quotations in this publication, unless otherwise indicated, are from the New Revised Standard Version of the Bible, copyrighted © by the Division of Christian Education of the National Council of the Churches of Christ in the United States of America, and are used by permission. All rights reserved.

For permission to reproduce any material in this publication, call 615-749-6421, or write to Cokesbury, Syndication—Permissions Office, 201 Eighth Avenue, South, P. O. Box 801, Nashville, Tennessee 37202.

To order copies of this publication, call toll free: 1-800-672-1789. Call Monday–Friday, 7:30–5:00 Central Time or 8:30–4:30 Pacific Time. Use your Cokesbury account, American Express, Visa, Discover, or MasterCard.

11 12 13 14 —— 20 19 18

EDITORIAL TEAM
Debra G. Ball-Kilbourne,
 Editor
Linda H. Leach,
 Assistant Editor
Linda Spicer,
 Adult Section
 Assistant

DESIGN TEAM
Susan J. Scruggs,
 Design Supervisor,
 Cover Design
Teresa B. Travelstead,
 Layout Designer

ADMINISTRATIVE STAFF
Neil M. Alexander,
 Vice-President,
 Publishing
Duane A. Ewers,
 Editor of Church School
 Publications
Gary L. Ball-Kilbourne,
 Executive Editor of
 Adult Publications

Art: Pat Bridges,
 pp. 22, 39, 78

TABLE OF CONTENTS

Volume 9: Matthew by Van Bogard Dunn

2		INTRODUCTION TO THE SERIES
3	Chapter 1	THE BIRTH OF JESUS THE MESSIAH: EMMANUEL
11	Chapter 2	THE BAPTISM AND TEMPTATION OF JESUS THE MESSIAH: SON OF GOD
19	Chapter 3	THE MINISTRY OF JESUS THE MESSIAH: PREACHING
27	Chapter 4	THE MINISTRY OF JESUS THE MESSIAH: TEACHING
35	Chapter 5	THE MINISTRY OF JESUS THE MESSIAH: HEALING
43	Chapter 6	THE MINISTRY OF JESUS THE MESSIAH ACCEPTED: AUTHORITY TO PREACH AND HEAL
51	Chapter 7	THE MINISTRY OF JESUS THE MESSIAH REJECTED: BLASPHEMY AGAINST THE HOLY SPIRIT
59	Chapter 8	THE MINISTRY OF JESUS THE MESSIAH MISUNDERSTOOD: THE NECESSITY OF THE CROSS
67	Chapter 9	THE MINISTRY OF JESUS THE MESSIAH DENIED: THE GRIEF OF SELF-RELIANCE
75	Chapter 10	THE MINISTRY OF JESUS THE MESSIAH AFFIRMED: THE PRAISE OF BABIES
83	Chapter 11	THE MINISTRY OF JESUS THE MESSIAH NOW AND NOT YET: THE COMING JUDGMENT
91	Chapter 12	THE MINISTRY OF JESUS THE MESSIAH COMPLETED: AGONY AND TRIUMPH
99	Chapter 13	THE MINISTRY OF JESUS THE MESSIAH CONTINUED: COMMISSION AND PROMISE
109		GLOSSARY
Inside back cover		MAP: PALESTINE IN JESUS' TIME

INTRODUCTION TO THE SERIES

Welcome to JOURNEY THROUGH THE BIBLE!
You are about to embark on an adventure that can change your life.

WHAT TO BRING WITH YOU
Don't worry about packing much for your trip. All you need to bring with you on this journey are
- an openness to God speaking to you in the words of Scripture
- companions to join you on the way, and
- your Bible

ITINERARY
In each session of this volume of JOURNEY THROUGH THE BIBLE, first you will be offered some hints for what to look for as you read the Bible text, and then you will be guided through four "dimensions" of study. Each is intended to help you through a well-rounded appreciation and application of the Bible's words.

HOW TO PREPARE FOR YOUR JOURNEY THROUGH THE BIBLE
Although you will gain much if all you do is show up for Bible study and participate willingly in the session, you can do a few things to gain even more:
- Read in advance the Bible passage mentioned in What to Watch For, using the summaries and hints as you read.
- During your Bible reading, answer the questions in Dimension 1.
- Read the rest of the session in this study book.
- Try a daily discipline of reading the Bible passages suggested in Dimension 4. Note that the Bible texts listed in Dimension 4 do *not* relate to a particular session. But if you continue with this daily discipline, by the end of thirteen weeks, you will have read through *all* of that portion of the Bible covered by this volume.

Studying the Bible is a lifelong project. JOURNEY THROUGH THE BIBLE provides you with a guided tour for a few of the steps along your way. May God be with you on your journey!

Gary L. Ball-Kilbourne
Executive Editor, Adult Publications
Church School Publications

Questions or comments?
Call Curric-U-Phone 1-800-251-8591.

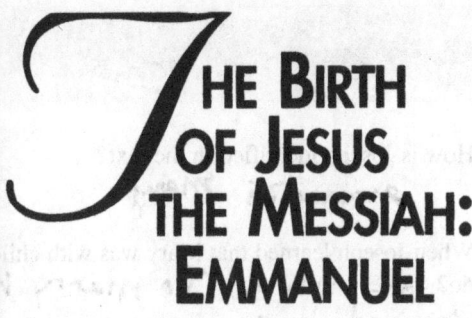

1 THE BIRTH OF JESUS THE MESSIAH: EMMANUEL

Matthew 1:18-25

What to Watch For

This session focuses on Matthew 1:18-25. In order to set the biblical material in its larger context, read Matthew 1:1-25. As you read, watch for these emphases:
- Jesus is the center of attention.
- Jesus is more significant than Abraham or David.
- The promises made to Abraham and to David are fulfilled in Jesus the Messiah (Christ).
- God's promises are fulfilled when God's people respond obediently to God's commands.
- Jesus is son of Abraham and son of David by virtue of his adoption by Joseph.
- The agent of God's action in the birth of Jesus by Mary is the Holy Spirit.
- The agent of God's action in the adoption of Jesus by Joseph is an angel of the Lord.
- The central theme of this passage, the promise of God contained in the name *Emmanuel* ("God is with us"), finds fulfillment in Jesus' birth.

In this session you will experience anew the fulfillment of God's promise to be with us as you reflect upon the witness of Matthew 1:18-25. This session presents a familiar passage and suggests new challenges and fresh understandings.

Dimension 1: What Does the Bible Say?

1. How is Joseph identified in the text?
   engaged to Mary

2. When Joseph learned that Mary was with child, what did he plan to do?
   He planned to marry her & then divorce her

3. What prevented his doing what he had planned?
   He had a dream. An angel of the Lord told him to marry her & to name him Jesus

4. Where does the prophecy concerning Emmanuel occur in the Hebrew Bible?

Dimension 2: What Does the Bible Mean?

Jesus the Messiah

The genealogy in Matthew 1:1-17 provides the backdrop for the affirmation in Matthew 1:18-25. Jesus is the anointed king—son of Abraham and son of David—whose function is to save his people from their sins. The claim that he is the Messiah—the Anointed One—does not arise because of the ordinary lineage from Abraham through King David. Rather the point for Matthew is the extraordinary conception in Mary by the Holy Spirit.

Jesus' miraculous birth equips him for his special ministry. His birth reveals how God intervenes in human history to bring the promise of salvation to fulfillment. Although the emphasis falls clearly upon God's action, however, the fulfillment of promised salvation always involves and requires human response.

The biblical text tells us nothing about the details of Jesus' conception. The text affirms simply that Mary was found to be with child (18). This passage is not complete until "she had borne a son" (25). Without Mary's womb, there would have been no Jesus the Messiah.

This passage addresses the understanding of some first century Jews that God's intervention in human history was a divine act so complete in itself that no human response was necessary. Some Jews claimed to be physical descendants of Abraham and David and therefore believed themselves to be without need of salvation from their sins. Others claimed that they needed to do nothing for salvation from their sins except to wait for God's miraculous intervention. In both of these cases, the result was a fatalistic determinism that encouraged people to ignore the salvation offered in the birth of Jesus the Messiah.

> ## WOMEN AND MATTHEW'S GOSPEL
>
> History in the ancient world was largely written from a male point of view. Roles of females were ignored or played down. Mary did not speak in this text. Yet Matthew did not entirely forget her. Her silent presence witnessed powerfully to the fact that in the Jesus movement women were the equal of men as the actors in God's drama of salvation. The text confronts the reader with the undeniable fact that, without unnamed and silent women, there would have been no people of God and no genealogy of Jesus the Messiah.
>
> Women were systematically excluded from leadership roles in the church. Men received the primary roles of leadership.
>
> However, in both the genealogy presented in Matthew 1:1-17 and the narrative in Matthew 1:18-25, an opposing tradition was present. Without the dramatic intervention of God in the lives of Tamar (1:3), Rahab (1:5), Ruth (1:5), and the wife of Uriah (1:6), the genealogy of the Messiah would have been disrupted. These four women prepare the reader for the central role that Mary played in the birth of the Messiah. Along with Mary they may have appeared in the text at this point as a warning to the reader: Resist the movement to exclude women from leadership roles in the continuing history of the Jesus community.

Joseph, Son of David

The action of the narrative unfolded around the character of Joseph. When Mary was discovered "before they lived together . . . to be with child from the Holy Spirit" (18), her fate depended upon Joseph because she had been engaged to him. As Mary's husband, Joseph had a legal right to expose her publicly as an adulteress and to see her punished, perhaps even put to death by stoning. Or Joseph could have quietly divorced her and left her to fend for herself in a hostile and suspicious community. In doing either, his action would have broken the genealogy of Jesus and made it impossible to proclaim Jesus as son of Abraham and son of David, the Messiah.

Matthew defined Joseph's role not by his legal and contractual rights as Mary's husband, but by his vocation as "son of David" (20). A revelation prevented Joseph from doing what he had planned. "An angel of the Lord appeared to him in a dream" (20). The angel reminded Joseph who he was—"son of David." The revelation freed Joseph from bondage to public opinion and to the limitations of his own righteousness: "Do not be afraid to take Mary as your wife, for the child conceived in her is from the Holy Spirit" (20). Furthermore, the revelation told Joseph what he had to do: "Take Mary as your wife.... you are to name [the son] Jesus" (20-21).

The angel of the Lord called Joseph to turn away from the pressures to conform to society and his own will. Instead he was instructed to trust in God. To be a son of David was more than physical descent. It resulted ultimately from living faithfully or obediently to God's extraordinary self-disclosure in the ordinary events of human life: engagement, marriage, conception, birth, naming, and sleep. Joseph was a son of David not because of his membership in an exclusive racial or religious group but because of his obedience to the angel of the Lord: "When Joseph awoke from sleep, he did as the angel of the Lord commanded him; he took her as his wife, but had no marital relations with her until she had borne a son; and he named him Jesus" (24-25).

Matthew's church was under heavy pressure to conform to the expectations of the surrounding society. If Matthew's church was located in northern Syria, perhaps in the city of Antioch (as many scholars believe), it was subject to the influence of a mixed racial, religious, and cultural population. Because of that congregation's origin in Judaism, it would have wanted to maintain a positive relationship with the Jewish religious tradition. Because of its commission to "make disciples of all nations" (28:19), that church would have felt committed to keep in touch with the various elements of the Gentile world. The danger from both Jewish and Gentile influences was that the church would lose its own identity and become nothing more than a reflection of the surrounding population.

Joseph's faithfulness modeled for the church how to live obediently in the world. As long as the church lived in primary relationship to God, it would escape the pressure to conform to society. As such, the church was made up of persons who, regardless of racial, religious, or cultural heritage, were sons and daughters of God because of the miraculous intervention of God in their lives.

Emmanuel, "God Is With Us"

In this passage, prophecy is fulfilled to give Mary's son the name *Emmanuel* in addition to the name *Jesus*. The name *Emmanuel* is unusual. Only here does the name occur in the entire New Testament. It is composed of the Hebrew words *immanu* ("with us") and *el* ("God").

The source of the Matthew 1:23 quotation in the Hebrew Bible is Isaiah 7:14. Although the meaning of Isaiah's passage during the reign of King Ahaz in 735 B.C. is difficult to determine, the Christian community that produced the Gospel of Matthew clearly understood it as a promise fulfilled by the birth of Jesus the Messiah. Reflection upon the traditions concerning the birth of Jesus led the church to a new understanding of the name *Emmanuel*. The prophecy did not determine the birth of Jesus. The birth of Jesus revealed what had only been dimly or partially grasped in the words of Isaiah: "Look, the young woman is with child and shall bear a son, and shall name him Immanuel" (Isaiah 7:14).

> **Emmanuel**
> [i-man'yoo-uhl] The symbolic name of a child whose birth, foretold by Isaiah, would be a sign to King Ahab that the Lord would deliver Israel from its enemies. In Matthew's Gospel Jesus is identified as Emmanuel, which literally means "with us [is] God." Jesus' birth is interpreted as the ultimate fulfillment of God's promise to deliver humankind from sin.

Jesus was understood as the embodiment of the name *Emmanuel* because in his vocation—"to save his people from their sins" (Matthew 1:21)—he manifested the presence of God. God was present to the people not as an overwhelming supernatural power but as the son born of Mary. God was with them in the sense that Jesus was one of them. He participated fully in their humanity. In his humanity he revealed to them who God was and who they were called to become. The miraculous birth of Jesus the Messiah from the Holy Spirit had only one purpose: to reveal how God was present to save people from their sins.

However, within Matthew's church, people continued to live as if God were not with them in Jesus. Matthew could observe divisions within the church, failure to keep the faith under pressure from the surrounding culture, anxiety about the present and the future, and attempts to find security by depending upon something other than God's presence. The church was far from perfect. Fallible and weak human beings, who were struggling daily with the realities of sin in their lives, made up the church. Jesus—Emmanuel—offered them salvation from their sins, but not by changing them into superhuman beings or by taking them out of the realities of human existence. He did so by being with them and by revealing to them that God was present with them. He provided all that they needed.

Jesus was the Messiah, son of Abraham, son of David, and Emmanuel because of his vocation. He qualified by his miraculous birth for that vocation. Likewise the people of Matthew's church were children of God because of their vocation. They qualified for that vocation by Emmanuel, God's miraculous presence in their lives.

What was the vocation or calling of the children of God? Joseph gave that answer in his response to the revelation of the angel of the Lord. They were called to obey the commands of God, to welcome Jesus into their homes, and to claim him as their very own. The promise of Emmanuel—God with us—always awaits fulfillment in the response of the children of God to their calling. The essence of faith is to live in the world as if all that matters is Emmanuel, God with us.

Dimension 3: What Does the Bible Mean to Us?

Matthew 1:18-25 challenges us to reflect upon how God is still present with us to save us from our sins. Our study of Matthew's witness to the birth of Jesus the Messiah should guide us toward receiving him into our lives as our Emmanuel, the fulfillment of God's promise to be with us.

Emmanuel, Our Judge

Often we do not conform our lives to God's purposes. We do not obey God's commands. We do not welcome the homeless and the outcast into our homes and claim them as members of our families. We forget that we are children of God, not because of our religious heritage, not because of our racial origin, not because of our national identity, but because of God's extraordinary intervention in our lives. We forget that our place in the household of God is a gift of God's grace by which we are enabled to become members of God's family. Emmanuel, our judge, is God present with us to save us from the sins of religious bigotry, racial pride, and national arrogance.

The birth of Jesus brings good news that God does not leave us to perish in our sins. Those who welcome him as their judge will know the joy of receiving him as their savior. The judgment of Emmanuel usually comes as a surprise, coming when we least expect it and from an unlikely source.

> Just as Joseph experienced an inner conflict between what his society and sense of morality required him to do on the one hand, and what the angel of the Lord commanded him to do on the other, so too must we make hard choices.

Several months ago a friend of mine told me of her experience hosting a pastor from Africa in her home. She assumed he would be radically different from her because of his racial and cultural background. She worried about the proper way to receive him. Seeing her effort to be sensitive to his special needs as a stranger in her home, he looked intently at her and said quietly, "In the heart we are all one." As my friend told me of this conversation, she affirmed Emmanuel who frees us from our assumed differences.

Experiencing Emmanuel makes us aware of the conflicts in our lives. Most of us would rather avoid this painful experience. Only by denying the presence of God in our lives can we avoid it, however. We sometimes must choose between what is customary and legal and what God calls us to do. The fact that we struggle with choices that require us to respond to God in ways that are often in conflict with our conditioned sense of "right" demonstrates the grace of God's judgment in our lives.

Emmanuel, Our Savior

Our basic sin is that we do not practice the presence of God. We live as if God were not present with us. This sin shows itself in different ways. Perhaps most tragically, we see it in aimless and purposeless existence. We may not be idle but we are busy with concerns and tasks that have no ultimate meaning. Therefore, these tasks never give us enduring satisfaction.

But meaning comes to our lives in the coming of Emmanuel. Emmanuel is our savior. In his birth we experience our calling from God to welcome the weak and the helpless into our lives, claiming them as members of our households.

Recently I spoke to a young man who is on the staff of a homeless shelter. I asked him how he came to be involved in such work. He told me that he had been a public relations officer for a luxury hotel. Increasingly, he felt dissatisfied with his employment, finding greater meaning in his work with the homeless. He said, "My work with these people, listening to them, caring for them, has opened my eyes to the fact that we are all kin. We have the same fears, the same hungers, the same ambitions. If I turned away from them and refused to welcome them as my kinfolk, I would be denying my own identity as a child of God." His words reminded me that the birth of the Messiah saves us from our sins by calling us to service, to be who we really are—children of God.

Emmanuel, Our Companion

The birth of the Messiah is more than a historic event. It witnesses to the experience of faith in the past, present, and future.

God's promise of Emmanuel helps us to remember that God's presence in our history has brought us to this moment. It also makes us aware that God is the living reality in whom we exist. Finally it assures us that no matter what the future holds, God is already there providing for all that we need.

The promise of God does not deny the uncertainty of human existence nor the fragility of life itself. The promise declares that the Companion who created our faith in the past and sustains it in the present will never fail us in the future. Those who receive Jesus into their lives as Emmanuel witness to this promise.

A friend was suffering from a mysterious pain and consulted with his physician. The physician ran a battery of tests, all of which had negative results. Then he recommended a CAT scan, a more sophisticated testing procedure.

As he waited for the scheduled CAT scan, my friend became more and more fearful. He described to me how lonely and helpless he felt as he arrived for the test.

In the midst of the procedure, however, my friend experienced a Presence that relieved his anxiety and filled him with a sense of well-being. He told me later, "During the CAT scan, with the clicking of the technology to remind me of the mystery surrounding me, I began to repeat one of the promises of my faith, 'Remember, I am with you always, to the end of the age' [Matthew 28:20]. And then I understood more fully than ever before what it means to call Jesus 'Emmanuel.'"

Dimension 4:
A Daily Bible Journey Plan

Day 1: Matthew 1:1-17
Day 2: Matthew 1:18-25
Day 3: Matthew 2:1-12
Day 4: Matthew 2:13-23
Day 5: Matthew 3:1-12
Day 6: Matthew 3:13–4:11
Day 7: Matthew 4:12-22

2 THE BAPTISM AND TEMPTATION OF JESUS THE MESSIAH: SON OF GOD

Matthew 3:13-17 4:1-11

What to Watch For

This session contains two episodes important for understanding the ministry of Jesus as presented by Matthew: the baptism (3:13-17) and the temptation (4:1-11). Watch for these events as you read the text in your Bible:

- Jesus responded to John's preaching by coming to him from Galilee to be baptized (13).
- John seemed to misunderstand Jesus because he thought that Jesus did not need baptism (14).
- Jesus rebuked John and submitted to baptism to "fulfill all righteousness" (15).
- Jesus' baptism opened the heavens, brought the Spirit of God to him, and won the approval of God: "This is my Son, the Beloved, with whom I am well pleased" (17).
- Jesus' relationship to God was tested in the wilderness by Satan (4:1).
- Jesus was tempted to use his relationship to God to satisfy his hunger, to protect himself from harm, and to realize personal ambition (3-8).
- Jesus resisted Satan by submitting to the word of God (10).

This session seeks to help you understand Jesus' baptism as his response to God's call to service and his temptation as his victory over self-service by obeying God's word.

Dimension 1: What Does the Bible Say?

1. Why did John try to prevent Jesus' baptism?

   He thought Jesus did not need to be baptized

2. Why did God approve Jesus' baptism?

   It fulfilled all righteousness

3. What are the connecting links between Jesus' baptism and his temptation?

4. How did Jesus resist the temptation of Satan?

Dimension 2: What Does the Bible Mean?

The report of Jesus' baptism in the Gospel of Matthew shows us God's viewpoint. The voice from heaven was God's voice. God gave Jesus the title of choice that took precedence over every other title. Note that Jesus was not addressed by God or by anyone in the Gospel of Matthew as "Son of God" until he was baptized by John. This fact implies that Jesus' divine sonship was revealed in his baptism and must be understood in light of his baptism. Just as his miraculous birth was associated with his vocation to "save his people from their sins" (12:1), so his relationship to God as Beloved Son was linked to his baptism at the hands of John the Baptist.

John's Ministry

Matthew presented a positive picture of the ministry of John the Baptist. John's message was essentially the message Jesus himself delivered: "Repent, for the kingdom of heaven has come near" (Matthew 3:2; Matthew 4:17). John's ministry fulfilled the prophecy of Isaiah 40:3. His preaching prepared the way for God to bring salvation to the people of Israel. John's raiment and diet signal Matthew's readers that Elijah had returned in John to begin God's promised redemption.

The identification of John as John *the Baptist* emphasized the fact that response to John's preaching led persons to want to be baptized by him. Gentiles converting to Judaism commonly were baptized as a rite of initiation. John may have gained the title *the Baptist* because he baptized Jews.

John called all Jews to baptism as an act of repentance. According to John's preaching all Jews were in need of God's salvation from sins. Further, the Lord's way required them to confess their sins.

John denounced the Pharisees and Sadducees as a "brood of vipers" because they came for baptism without bearing "fruit worthy of repentance" (3:7-8). Repentance meant more than desire to escape God's judgment on evil deeds. More fundamentally, repentance also meant a turning to God in the realization that repentance depended upon the goodness of God.

Although the text focuses upon the Jews, the text clearly implies that the distinction between Jews and Gentiles had already been removed. Lineage does not make a person a child of Abraham; the grace of God that calls one to repentance and empowers the bearing of "fruit worthy of repentance" makes a person a child of Abraham. The same God who acted miraculously in the history of Israel to fulfill the promise of salvation now acted in John's ministry to bring that history to fulfillment. However, John warned that only those who bore the "fruit worthy of repentance" would receive the joy of the kingdom of heaven. All others would be "cut down and thrown into the fire" (3:9-10).

Although Matthew favorably presented John's ministry, John was a lesser figure than Jesus. John's function was to point away from himself toward the one who was more powerful and more worthy. John's ministry awaited the fulfillment of the one coming after him and authentically witnessed to that one. John's preaching and baptizing occurred for the sake of something greater.

Conflict surfaced when John attempted to prevent Jesus from being baptized. John presumed to tell Jesus how to act. John had a different understanding than Jesus about what was appropriate for one more powerful and more worthy. Perhaps John expected Jesus to carry on his public ministry as the agent of God's final judgment upon all who have disobeyed God. From John's point of view, it was not proper for the judge of all creation to participate in a baptism offered to sinners. John expected Jesus to "gather his wheat [the righteous] into the granary" and to burn "the chaff" (the unrighteous) "with unquenchable fire" (3:12).

John was right, of course, to identify Jesus as the judge of the end time; he was wrong to expect Jesus to act as the judge before the end had come. John did not know what time it was. Since he did not know the time, he was mistaken about what Jesus ought to do.

Jesus' Vocation

Matthew's narrative of Jesus' baptism clarified Jesus' vocation. Jesus responded to the preaching of John and was baptized by John because he experienced the call of God to a life of service.

The dialogue between John and Jesus at the Jordan (3:13-15) was about the nature of repentance. John was right to assume that Jesus did not need to repent of his sins. He properly said to Jesus, "I need to be baptized by you, and do you come to me?" (14). However, John missed the point by not comprehending that repentance involves turning to God, centering one's life in God, and accepting the will of God as the supreme good of one's life. Therefore, Jesus did what was appropriate *now*. Jesus turned to God in absolute dependence upon God and claimed for himself the vocation announced in the story of his miraculous birth: "He will save his people from their sins. . . . And they shall name him Emmanuel . . . God is with us" (1:21, 23).

> Righteousness is behavior conforming to the laws that define what is right. Since the laws of right behavior come from God, righteousness is a right relationship to God made manifest in right action. Jesus' baptism fulfilled "all righteousness" because his right relationship to God (his dependence upon God) was revealed in his right action (his obedience to God). Right action requires and results from a right relationship to God. (3:2)

John saw Jesus as the one who comes to judge at the end of time. Instead, Jesus was more powerful and more worthy than John. Jesus was the one in whom the salvation of "the kingdom of heaven has come near." Because Jesus submitted to the rule of God in his life, in him the promises of God to the people of God are fulfilled. Therefore, Jesus corrected John and declared his life's work by accepting John's baptism, "Let it be so now; for it is proper for us in this way to fulfill all righteousness" (3:15). The key word in this passage is *righteousness*.

The unusual events that occurred after Jesus' baptism underscore the importance of the baptism for Jesus' life and ministry. That "the heavens were opened to him" (3:16) indicated that his obedience to God had given Jesus direct access to the presence of God in his life. His vision of "the Spirit of God descending like a dove and alighting on him" made him aware of the power of God available to him for the fulfillment of his ministry. The voice from heaven saying, "This is my Son, the Beloved, with whom I am well pleased" (17) gave him the assurance that he had found favor with God by choosing the will of God as the ultimate good of his life.

These unusual events at his baptism also emphasize that Jesus' right relationship to God brought him to a right relationship with the children of God, his sisters and brothers. He had come from Galilee to the Jordan with "the people of Jerusalem and all Judea . . . and all the region along the Jordan" (5). They were all sinners, "confessing their sins" (6). The narrative proclaims that Jesus, son of Abraham, son of David, born of Mary from the Holy Spirit, is the Son of God, in whom God is with God's people to save them from their sins. He left everything to be with them in their sins and therefore, he is the one in whom they experience Emmanuel, "God is with us."

Jesus' Temptation

The temptation of Jesus directly followed his baptism. The Spirit that he saw "descending like a dove and alighting on him" led him "into the wilderness to be tempted by the devil" (Matthew 4:1). So the power of God did not remove Jesus from the struggle against evil but brought him face to face with the embodiment of evil.

Jesus prepared for the engagement by fasting forty days and forty nights" (2). He focused his attention upon God and centered his life completely in God's will. Drawing near to God did not make Jesus less human. Rather he seemed more human as he experienced his own hunger.

That which was at stake in Jesus' temptation in the wilderness was a decision about what he valued most highly. The devil represented the power of deception seeking to convince Jesus that his hunger as the Son of God could be satisfied by something other than his obedience to God's will. The temptation tested him to determine whether he would deny his divine sonship. Would Jesus use his divine sonship to satisfy his own desires? Or would he confirm it by realizing it more fully in obedience to God?

> The baptism revealed Jesus as the Son of God.

Each encounter with the deception of the devil confronted Jesus with a hunger and with a decision:

- The temptation to turn stones into loaves of bread was powerful because it offered immediate gratification of physical hunger (4:3-4).
- The temptation to throw himself down from the pinnacle of the Temple required Jesus to choose between attracting attention to himself or by submitting to the will of God. But hunger for fame is not what drove his life. Hunger for God was the consuming passion of his life, taking precedence over every other desire and setting him free from the deceit of seeking to save his life. He triumphed over the illusion of personal fame because he chose to make the will of God for his life more important than a miraculous rescue from danger (5-7).
- The temptation to worship the devil and to receive the kingdoms of the world was the climax to Jesus' struggle to overcome deceit in the wilderness of his hunger. What was worthy of the ultimate allegiance of his life? Jesus was *spiritually* hungry. He found it impossible to live only within himself. He had to worship and serve something greater than himself. He would be the son of the power he chose to serve. The voice of deceit had no power over him because he listened to the word of God, the voice of truth. The devil was now called by name, *Satan*, which literally means "adversary." By relying upon the truth of the word of God, Jesus banished the adversarial deceit and falsehood of Satan from his life. Jesus acknowledged and satisfied the deepest hunger of his life as he worshiped the Lord his God and served only him (8-10).

These texts about the baptism and temptation of Jesus show that Jesus was proclaimed as Son of God because he accepted his vocation from God and fulfilled his vocation by worshiping and serving God alone. The promises of God were not fulfilled in Jesus in a fatalistic and mechanical fashion. Rather Jesus made a dynamic and liberating decision about his ultimate allegiance. Matthew says to Gospel readers that they can only come to accept Jesus as God's Son, the Beloved, by entering into his baptism; participating in his temptation; and by experiencing anew how he is Emmanuel, God with us, saving his people from the deceit of Satan.

Dimension 3: What Does the Bible Mean to Us?

These two stories about the baptism and temptation of Jesus are important resources for us as we seek to live faithfully today. We see in them how Jesus reveals the presence of God in our lives and empowers us to respond obediently to God's will.

God Is With Us in Our Baptism and Our Temptation

The stories about Jesus' baptism and temptation tell us primarily about God. As Matthew tells the stories, God does not wait for human beings to take the initiative. Rather God is already present in our lives, seeking us before we are aware of God's action. The details in the texts showing us this fact are the following:

- Jesus came to John to be baptized.
- Jesus overcame John's attempt to prevent his baptism.
- Jesus' action was accompanied by God's actions: the heavens were opened, the Spirit of God descended, God named Jesus "Beloved Son."
- The Spirit led Jesus to be tempted by the devil.
- Jesus was able to resist Satan because he was guided by God's word.
- Angels came and waited on Jesus after he banished Satan.

Although these texts are not about our baptisms and our temptations, they help us to see how God is with us in our baptisms and temptations.

A few days ago I was present at the baptism of an infant in our church. Thoughts about these baptism and temptation texts ran through my mind as I watched the ritual and participated in the liturgy. I realized that the child's baptism was not a celebration of our acts or our words but a celebration of God's acts and God's words. What we did in the baptism was incomplete in the same way that John's preaching and baptism were incomplete. However, since Jesus had fulfilled "all righteousness" (Matthew 3:15) in his baptism, I knew that God was with the infant, with the parents, with the whole congregation, with all God's children.

> And a voice from heaven said, "This is my [child], the Beloved, with whom I am well pleased" (Matthew 3:16-17).

Reflection on this baptism reminded me that what we celebrate in baptism must always be realized in the wilderness of our temptations. To be a child of God means being fully human, experiencing hunger. All of us are led by the Spirit into situations where we must choose as Jesus chose between the words of deceit and the words of truth.

I began to imagine what awaited all of God's infants as they grow into maturity. No human being can live and grow without hunger. How we choose to satisfy our hunger is the ultimate test of our relationship to God. Words of deceit constantly bombard us. Powerful and persuasive voices teach us that our greatest good is to be found by seeking material wealth, public acclaim, and personal power.

How can a helpless child withstand these voices of deceit, live in dependence upon God, and fulfill all righteousness?

Only in obedience to the word of God, the voice of truth, do the children of God experience victory over the voices of deceit. Every baptism inevitably leads to the wilderness of temptation.

If the church is aware of what it claims for its children in baptism, then it must commit all of its resources to enabling all its children to hunger and thirst for righteousness. A church so committed will develop a vigorous program of education that helps children, youth, and adults to hear the word of God and to respond obediently.

God Is With Us to Give Us Victory Over Evil

These Bible texts are the ground of triumphant faith. They remind us that we have nothing to fear from the forces of evil because they have already been overcome by the power of God's love revealed in Jesus.

Are we helpless in the face of evil forces that threaten to overwhelm us? Recently I was caught in the midst of circumstances appearing to confirm the idea that evil is so powerful that we can do nothing to overcome it.

> We have nothing to fear from the forces of evil.

I am involved with a settlement house in the inner city located several miles from my home. One day when I arrived, all the members of the staff were gathered around their van. Obviously something dreadful had happened. Vandals had broken into the van and had deliberately caused over two thousand dollars worth of damage. I thought the staff members would be paralyzed by this senseless act of violence. Instead they were filled with concern for the persons who had committed the destruction.

As I listened to them discuss what had happened, I was surprised to learn that they spent very little time bewailing the loss of their property. Instead they focused on how they could find the guilty parties and help them become responsible members of the neighborhood. They were motivated to provide help for members of the community who were so alienated that they resorted to violent acts against an agency dedicated to helping them.

A few days later they found the three boys who had vandalized their van. They invited them to become members of an after-school group that met in the settlement house gym. I was present at the meeting of the group when the three boys were introduced.

The leader told what the boys had done and reminded the group that they all had done destructive things. The boys had joined the group because they were all members of the same community who needed support and encouragement to become responsible and constructive members of the community. The action of the boys was condemned as bad behavior but the boys were not condemned as bad boys. They were accepted into the group just as others had been accepted. They were expected to respect the rules that made it possible for members of the group to work and play together.

No one could guarantee that the three boys would become responsible members of the group, but the group had decided to give them a chance instead of excluding them. The group also had resisted the temptation to become vengeful and self-righteous. It had demonstrated in its own life the power that overcomes evil.

The stories of Jesus' baptism and temptation show us that we are given opportunities to join with Jesus in accepting our own call to service. God is always present in our lives offering us the choices to satisfy the deepest hungers of our lives. We are not puppets on a string, and God is not the puppeteer. We are responsible human beings who must make real choices. Often our choices are made in confusing circumstances. We may be deceived by what seems to satisfy our hunger: material wealth, public acclaim, and personal power. But when we make our choices in the light of Jesus' example and in response to the word of God, we see clearly that we are children of God, empowered and supported by God to fulfill all righteousness. We discover that evil no longer has power over us. We have chosen to live in dependence upon the self-giving love of God revealed in Jesus, our Emmanuel.

Dimension 4:
A Daily Bible Journey Plan

Day 1: Matthew 4:23–5:16
Day 2: Matthew 5:17-26
Day 3: Matthew 5:27-32
Day 4: Matthew 5:33-42
Day 5: Matthew 5:43-48
Day 6: Matthew 6:1-15
Day 7: Matthew 6:16-24

3 THE MINISTRY OF JESUS THE MESSIAH: PREACHING

Matthew 4:12-25

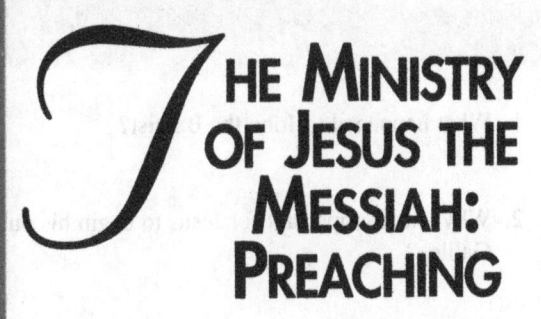

What to Watch For

Jesus was the one who was mightier than John the Baptist, worthy of the ultimate allegiance of the people. Jesus now began his public ministry after John had been removed from the scene.

In the Gospel of Matthew readers can see that Jesus fulfilled all of God's promises. The time of preparation announced by John the Baptist now gave way to the time of accomplishment in the life and ministry of Jesus.

As you read Matthew 4:12-25, watch for these items:
- Jesus moved from Nazareth to Capernaum.
- Jesus' ministry included Jews and Gentiles.
- Jesus preached the same message John preached: "Repent, for the kingdom of heaven has come near" (17).
- Jesus called people to leave their ordinary routine and to follow him.
- Jesus promised to make his followers "fish for people" (19).
- Jesus called his followers to leave everything: work, relationships, and property.
- Jesus brought "the good news of the kingdom" (23) to the crowds who followed him.

In this section receive the preaching of Jesus as the "good news of the kingdom."

Dimension 1: What Does the Bible Say?

1. What happened to John the Baptist?

2. Why was it important for Jesus to begin his public ministry in Galilee?

3. What did Jesus mean when he promised that he would make his followers "fish for people"?

4. What was the difference between John's ministry and Jesus' ministry?

Dimension 2: What Does the Bible Mean?

Matthew presented Jesus as the one whose ministry embodied "the good news of the kingdom" (23). These words do not define the life and ministry of Jesus; the life and ministry of Jesus define the words. *Gospel* literally means "good news." This good news is the fact that Jesus is Emmanuel, God with us. Everything Matthew recorded about the life and ministry of Jesus in the rest of his Gospel elaborates on the meaning of this phrase, *the good news of the kingdom.*

Good News for Evil Times

At every critical moment in his ministry, Jesus made a decision based upon his vocation. The brief reference in Matthew 4:12 to John's arrest alerts us to the conflict present as the kingdom of heaven draws near. The kingdom of heaven represented by John and by Jesus challenged every other ruling authority. It required people to choose under whose rule they would live: God's or that of those authorities seemingly in charge. John's arrest illustrated the conflict between God's truth and Satan's falsehood within world history. To choose to live under God's authority inevitably provoked hostility from lesser authorities such as King Herod.

King Herod *seemed* to have absolute authority over his subjects. His word was law; what he said was done. John was arrested because he chose to live by God's law instead of Herod's. His fate was sealed by that choice. John *appeared* to be at the disposal of King Herod's unlimited authority.

But appearance and reality are two different things. John chose the only authentic authority, the authority of God. Therefore, no matter to what degree he seemed to be under the control of King Herod, he actually was protected by God from all that King Herod could do. John did not fear King Herod who could kill his body but could not kill his soul; rather he feared God who could destroy both soul and body in hell (10:26-28).

FOR MORE INFORMATION ABOUT JOHN THE BAPTIST, READ MATTHEW 11:2-19 AND 14:1-12.

Jesus began his ministry aware of the consequences of his own choices. When he "heard that John had been arrested" (4:12), Jesus knew that what had happened to John awaited him also. Jesus revealed his ultimate allegiance in his baptism and temptation. He also showed it in his choice of residence. He established his home not with his family in Nazareth but in the city of his own choice, Capernaum. He "withdrew" to Galilee not to save his life but to respond to God's call.

Jesus' life and ministry embodied the good news of the Kingdom that God does not leave people to struggle alone against evil. God came to the people at the point of their need and revealed the power to overcome evil. That power was the self-giving love of the one who left everything to make his home among them so that they might receive the Kingdom and become sons and daughters of God.

No power could prevent the good news of the Kingdom from seeking people where they were. The evil power of King Herod was in fact powerless. Ordinary assumptions about authority and control were radically reversed. Those who seemed to have the last word because of their power to kill the body were revealed as impotent impostors. The one who seemed to be at the disposal of the agents of violence was revealed as God's last word because he found his life by losing it in humble service.

Good News for All

Over the ages some people have misunderstood God's promised salvation, thinking that it was for some people but not for all. Persons in Matthew's church might well have held such a narrow, exclusive understanding of the kingdom of heaven. Their misunderstanding may have assumed that God had chosen Israel for special privileges while excluding the Gentiles. Matthew insisted, however, that God's special choice of Israel always included Israel's special responsibility to be the agent of salvation for the Gentiles—for all nations.

Matthew was aware that the Hebrew Bible contained visions of God's salvation that included the Gentiles. Using the formula of prophecy and fulfillment already seen in Matthew 1 and 2, Matthew claimed that Isaiah 9:1-2 was fulfilled when Jesus made his home in Capernaum. Salvation for the Gentiles no longer was a future hope but now was a present reality because Jesus left Nazareth and established his dwelling in Capernaum. The verbs in the quotation from Isaiah declare that what was foretold by Isaiah had now become an accomplished fact.

"The people who sat in darkness
have seen a great light,
and for those who sat in the
region and shadow of death
light has dawned" (Matthew 4:16).

Matthew did not interpret Jesus in light of the Isaiah text. He came to his understanding of the Isaiah text as he reflected on his experience of Jesus as Emmanuel. Because in him the good news of the Kingdom was present, Jesus was the light for those who sat in darkness. Matthew saw Isaiah's words fulfilled as Jesus preached the good news of the Kingdom, called disciples, and healed the sick. "Great crowds followed him from Galilee, the Decapolis, Jerusalem, Judea, and from beyond the Jordan" (Matthew 4:25).

Good News for Disciples

Jesus designed his preaching of the good news of the Kingdom to create a community of followers or disciples. His message demanded more than assent to propositions. He called for a radical reorientation of one's life. God's action in the good news of the Kingdom made repentance possible. Humans appropriate the good news of the Kingdom by responding with repentance.

Matthew helped his readers understand how the gospel transforms people into disciples by reporting what happened to Simon, Andrew, James, and John when they encountered Jesus by the Sea of Galilee. Jesus acted first. Walking along the shore, he saw Simon and Andrew. Jesus spoke to Simon and Andrew: "Follow me, and I will make you fish for people" (19). Then seeing James and John, he called them as well.

To be sure, Simon, Andrew, James, and John responded to Jesus' action. Matthew wrote about Simon and Andrew: "Immediately they left their nets and followed him" (20) and about James and John: "Immediately they left the boat and their father, and followed him" (22). But the radical transformation of their lives was made possible by the one who came to them where they were and invited them to become more than they had dreamed of being.

Though they had no prior knowledge of Jesus, the four fishermen immediately and totally reordered their lives. They had not heard his teaching. Neither had they witnessed his acts of compassion or his mighty works.

Yet they left everything. Matthew did not explain why. He simply declared that they left their livelihood, their property, and their families to follow Jesus. They followed him not knowing where he was going. They only knew that in him they had met the one who had authority to lead.

> Discipleship is a human impossibility. Simon and Andrew did not find Jesus; Jesus found them.

What was the nature of that authority? By choosing the will of God as the ultimate good of his life, Jesus had embraced the authority of God as his own. Since Jesus wanted what God wanted, the four fishermen confronted in Jesus the will of God for their lives. They left everything behind because they had been claimed by what they really wanted: the good news of the Kingdom. Jesus' vocation gave them their own vocation. All the lesser goods of their lives—livelihood, property, and family—were subordinated to the one supreme good: the kingdom of heaven.

Jesus addressed these four persons by the Sea of Galilee as individuals. They were not numbers or faceless members of the crowd. They were real persons with specific names: Simon, Andrew, James, John. As individuals of infinite worth and dignity they were called to participate in a community of vision and purpose. The call to the service of the kingdom of heaven saved them from the routine of meaningless existence. In the community of Jesus' followers, they would share with him the work of the Kingdom. They would be a "great light" to the people who sat in darkness as the light dawning in Jesus reflected in them. What he did, they also would do. They, too, would proclaim the good news of the Kingdom in word and deed as they followed Jesus.

Dimension 3: What Does the Bible Mean to Us?

These passages from Matthew focus attention upon Jesus as the proclaimer or preacher of the good news of the Kingdom. They help us see that our life together in the church presupposes the gospel. Perhaps Matthew had seen in his church signs of disorder resulting from organizing the church around something other than the good news of the Kingdom. These texts become immediately relevant for us. They call us once again to heed the preaching of Jesus so that our lives together will be delivered from the signs of disorder and decline that are so tragically present today.

Good News for Evil Times

We are seldom challenged by powers so obviously as evil as King Herod. The expressions of evil in our own time usually are far more subtle.

> To whom or to what do you give your deepest allegiance?

Examine your own life in the light of the good news of the Kingdom. To whom or to what do you give your deepest allegiance? Do you sometimes claim to submit to the will of God while denying God's will by the choices you make?

Or look at the church and at society. Does the Herodian way of life—the way of violence, manipulation, and death—creep into our political institutions and transform them into agents of evil? In what ways has even the church become involved in Herodian attitudes and practices?

These questions disturb us because we find that we often "are the people who sat in darkness... who sat in the region and shadow of death" (16). Our need then is to hear the good news of the Kingdom and to live in hope grounded on the fact that we "have seen a great light" because "light has dawned."

I watched a retired African American public school teacher teaching a group of inner-city children the song, "This Little Light of Mine." She was a superb musician, a skilled teacher, an excellent communicator. In addition to all of those things that were the result of her training and experience, she also enjoyed a quality that was much more important. She embodied the good news of the Kingdom.

As I saw the radiance of her face and the shining eyes of the children gathered around her, I was reminded of the good news of the Kingdom: God is with us. God is with us when it seems that greed and callousness have overwhelmed the children. God is with us when we are tempted to conclude that nothing we do will make a difference. God is with us as the great light in Jesus ignites our little lights and keeps them shining in the darkness.

Good News for All

The good news of the Kingdom includes the Gentiles. That idea may not startle us because we have become so familiar with it. But until we are startled by it, we will not experience its demand upon our lives.

The word *Gentiles* (15) referred to the whole non-Jewish population of the world. For centuries the Jewish people had been taught that only those who practiced the Jewish religion could enter into a completely fulfilling relationship with God. Therefore non-Jews were excluded from the worship of God. They were also excluded from intimate social relationships, especially table fellowship, with practicing Jews. The only way non-Jews could enter the Jewish community was through circumcision and obedience to the laws of Judaism. The exclusion of non-Jews or Gentiles was a matter of religious principle.

The good news of the Kingdom as Jesus preached and embodied it included Jews and non-Jews solely on the basis of God's grace, freely given to all people. All were the same in the sight of God. We may experience the radical nature of an all-inclusive gospel when we consider what an all-inclusive gospel does not mean.

It does not mean that God includes only those who agree with us. It does not mean that God includes only those who behave the way we behave. It does not mean that God includes only those who think about God the way we think. It does not mean that God includes only those who participate in our culture. It does not mean that God includes only those with whom we are comfortable.

> The good news of the Kingdom as Jesus preached and embodied it included Jews and non-Jews solely on the basis of God's grace, freely given to all people.

I experienced the positive consequences of the good news of the Kingdom as I sat at a table with a young woman whose lifestyle threatened me by its strangeness. She was a chain smoker whose life journey included alcohol and drug addiction, rape, the bearing of two children before she was twenty, homelessness, and poverty.

A young man also sat at the same table. He had committed his life to reaching out and helping people in great need. He spoke to her easily, evoked her response, listened attentively, treated her with dignity and respect. As I listened to their conversation and was drawn into their sharing, I had to question my preconceptions and prejudices. Although I still find it difficult to accept the fact that all of us are equal before God, I cannot justify my tendency to exclude persons like this woman. Surely God has something better in store for us.

Good News for Disciples

Recently I received a letter from a woman whom I do not know. She wrote me because she wanted to share a part of her life story. It was a remarkable letter chiefly because of what she chose to tell me about what was really important to her.

She had married an ordained minister with whom she had lived and served for thirty-two years until his death. She described her husband as a faithful servant, a loving partner, and a devoted father. She mentioned the joy of their life together, the sorrow of his death, and the consolation of victory over death. As she closed the letter, she wrote that she now was teaching a Sunday school class.

Her letter forcefully reminded me that the good news of the Kingdom comes to us wherever we are. It offers us the opportunity to leave everything to become servants of the Kingdom. The humble service of those who have followed Jesus into the joy of meaningful work is one sign that the good news of the Kingdom has been heard. As I read the letter, I became aware of a woman who had done many of the same activities for much of her life and who had never journeyed far from home. Yet her life had not been routine. Nor had it been narrow and confined. It had been rich and rewarding, open and enlarging. Jesus had seen her, called her to become a member of his community, and challenged her by his promise. She had never changed her work or left her home but she *had* left everything and followed Jesus. Her testimony was the convincing witness of one whose life's work interpreted the words of Jesus, "Follow me, and I will make you fish for people."

Dimension 4: A Daily Bible Journey Plan

Day 1: Matthew 6:25-34
Day 2: Matthew 7:1-11
Day 3: Matthew 7:12-20
Day 4: Matthew 7:21-29
Day 5: Matthew 8:1-13
Day 6: Matthew 8:14-27
Day 7: Matthew 8:28-34

THE MINISTRY OF JESUS THE MESSIAH: TEACHING

Matthew 6:1-21

What to Watch For

This session looks at one of the central emphases of the Sermon on the Mount in Matthew 6:1-21. Jesus taught about the proper relationship to God and its reward. The following are some of the most important issues raised in the text:

- Righteousness is known only to God and rewarded by God.
- Righteousness includes giving alms, praying, and fasting.
- Hypocrites practice righteousness to be seen by people and rewarded by people.
- A right relationship to God results in a right relationship to people.
- Righteousness stores up everlasting treasure in heaven.
- Treasure in heaven belongs to those who desire it as their highest good.

> You may find it helpful to read the entire Sermon on the Mount, Matthew 5:1–7:29.

This session seeks to help you experience the reward of righteousness by hearing and doing the teaching of Jesus about giving alms, praying, and fasting.

27

Dimension 1: What Does the Bible Say?

1. Who rewards righteousness? *God*

2. What is the reward of righteousness? *Kingdom*

3. Who rewards the righteousness of hypocrites? *man*

4. What is the reward of the righteousness of hypocrites?

Dimension 2: What Does the Bible Mean?

Jesus went up on the mountain and sat down to teach his disciples and the crowds (Matthew 5:1). Matthew's first readers would have understood the symbolism. The mountain recalled Moses receiving the Law on Mount Sinai. Teachers sat as they taught their pupils. In the Sermon on the Mount, Jesus took over the role of teacher of the Law for his followers.

The Sermon on the Mount ended when the crowds, astounded by Jesus' teaching, recognized that "he taught them as one having authority, and not as their scribes" (7:28-29).

The Sermon on the Mount was for everyone. Everyone was a potential follower of Jesus. His teaching opened the "narrow gate" and the "hard road" that led to "life" so that the crowds might choose for themselves the kingdom of heaven as their supreme good (7:13-14).

Jesus had chosen his own vocation in the wilderness by relying upon the word of God for guidance. In the same way the disciples and crowds were given an opportunity to choose their vocation by relying upon the authoritative teaching of Jesus for guidance. The life one lived provided the evidence that one had learned the teachings of the Sermon on the Mount. Jesus intended in the Sermon on the Mount that the disciples and the crowds would hear and act on his words (7:21-27).

Practicing Righteousness

The Greek word translated as "piety" in Matthew 6:1 by the New Revised Standard Version is the same word translated as "righteousness" in the report of Jesus' baptism in Matthew 3:15. *Dikaiosune* means, in this context, the action that fulfills or meets the requirements of a person's relationship to God. Thus, to practice righteousness expresses a right relationship to God.

In order to be disciples or followers of Jesus, righteousness must not only be discussed; it must also be done. The three activities considered by Jesus as essential elements of righteousness are almsgiving, prayer, and fasting. All faithful Jews would have recognized these activities as required by their relationship to God.

Almsgiving

Almsgiving grew out of concern for the poor. This concern is evident throughout the Hebrew Bible, especially in laws on behalf of the poor such as Leviticus 19:10 and Deuteronomy 14:28. Hebrew laws addressing the plight of people ensnared in poverty assumed the unity of the people before God. These laws focused on the obligations of those persons who were not poor. The failure of affluent persons to live by those obligations created social inequality and injustice.

> The prophets spoke strongly against the abuse of the poor by the rich and condemned it as sin against God. Read Isaiah 5:8; Jeremiah 34:13-17; Amos 2:6-8; 3:15; 4:1; 5:11-12.

Since God is the God of all the people, to neglect the needs of the impoverished violates God's will for all the people. Such neglect reveals that the people as a whole are not in an acceptable relationship to God. Jesus drew upon Israel's social conscience when he taught his disciples that persons in a right relationship to God give alms.

Prayer

The amount of attention Jesus gave to the subject of prayer in the Sermon on the Mount shows that Jesus considered it a fundamental action of righteousness. Again Jesus taught from the basic teachings of the Hebrew Bible. Prayer included all the forms of communication people employed to praise and petition God. In prayer, persons spoke directly to God rather than talked about God. Prayer was personal, simple, and confident. Although prayer primarily praised God as Savior and Creator and petitioned for the coming of God's kingdom and justice, it also contained requests for the daily needs and desires of the people.

Jesus addressed God as "Father" in accordance with Jewish practice to express his strong faith in God's goodness and his dependence upon God's power. How a person prayed revealed how one understood God and one's responsibility before God. Therefore it was the most important indication of one's relationship to God.

Fasting

Fasting was related directly to prayer. In fasting, a person deliberately abstained from food and sometimes drink for a prolonged period as a means of acknowledging one's dependence upon God. The practice probably originated as a sign of mourning. Jews observed fasting during periods of penitence and to prepare for a divine revelation. The law of Moses required fasting only in connection with the observance of the Day of Atonement (Leviticus 16:29-31; 23-27). All other fast days were voluntary except those proclaimed in periods of national crisis. Fasts commemorated the destruction of Jerusalem and the Exile. They lasted for different periods of time: one day or one night, three days, seven days, or forty days. In the Christian church, weekly fasts became a regular practice on Wednesdays and Fridays. Jesus accepted fasting as a normal part of a righteous person's life.

> **Hypocrite** - Literally a stage actor. Jesus used it to condemn those who practiced their religion to pretend to be what they were not.

Righteousness of Hypocrites

In Matthew's church practicing righteousness had become a problem. Some persons gave alms, prayed, and fasted in a way that separated them from God instead of drawing them closer to God.

This problem was a matter of ultimate seriousness for Christians because the wrong practice of righteousness would deprive a person of God's reward—entering into the kingdom of heaven (Matthew 5:20; 6:33; 7:21-23).

People practicing righteousness in the wrong way were called "hypocrites."

Hypocrites revealed that their hearts were in the wrong place by what they did. They practiced their righteousness "before others in order to be seen by them" (6:1). When they gave alms, they sounded a trumpet to "be praised by others" (6:2). When they prayed, they sought to attract attention to themselves. When they fasted, they disfigured themselves so that others would know they were fasting. Because these otherwise spiritual actions were done in a self-serving manner, the behavior of hypocrites was spiritually destructive. They used their almsgiving, praying, and fasting as masks to hide what they really were and to make others accept them for what they pretended to be. Jesus portrayed them as negative role models whose practice of righteousness was to be avoided. He repeated the words *do not* throughout the lesson to focus attention upon the pattern of behavior that threatened to corrupt the faith community.

Hypocrites get what they earn. The phrase *they have received their reward* recurs throughout the passage as a grim warning that people receive as their reward what they seek as their supreme good. Hypocrites receive no reward from God in heaven.

Jesus' words compare the praise of others earned by hypocrites to earthly treasure. It is fleeting and fragile. Earthly treasure is exposed to moths, rust, and thieves. What happens to earthly treasure happens also to the reward of hypocrites because where their treasure is, there their hearts will be also.

> If you define your life in terms of that which has no enduring quality, you cannot expect to enjoy relationships with that which is eternal. Hypocrites perish with their treasure.

Righteousness of Disciples

Hypocrites show their inner disposition in *self*-serving action. Disciples, however, show their inner disposition in *God*-serving action. Jesus not only taught his disciples to avoid the "righteousness" of the hypocrites. He also taught them the righteousness to practice as his followers. He enjoined them to give alms spontaneously as the overflow of their true nature. He commanded them to pray as if they were alone before God, responding to God as freely as God communed with them. He instructed them to fast, not to impress others, but to focus their attention upon God and God's will for their lives. Others might not discern any difference in external appearance between the righteousness of hypocrites and that of disciples. But God sees and rewards the internal reality done "in secret."

The words *in secret* recur throughout the passage. Authentic righteousness assumed that the kingdom of heaven was the supreme good for all people which all would embrace when they experienced Jesus' life and ministry. The practice of righteousness was not the *condition* for receiving the kingdom of heaven but the *consequence* of receiving it. The secrecy in which the followers of Jesus gave alms, prayed, and fasted distinguished them. They did not work to earn the reward of the kingdom of heaven. They worked in response to the reward of the kingdom of heaven that they had received as the gift of God's goodness. Therefore, when they gave alms, prayed, and fasted, they responded to God's unconditional gift by giving themselves unconditionally to God and God's service.

Jesus sought to reveal the kingdom of heaven as the only treasure worthy of the heart's allegiance. No matter how a person practiced the externals of righteousness, if the heart was fixed on earthly treasure, that "righteousness" was hypocritical. No matter how one practiced the externals of righteousness, if the heart was fixed on heavenly treasure, that righteousness was genuine. "For where your treasure is, there your heart will be also" (6:21).

> Our Father who art in heaven, hallowed be thy name . . .

Jesus' teaching on prayer formed the center from which all his other teaching about righteousness arose. Whether prayer was private or public was irrelevant. Prayer only happened "in secret"—that is, centered on God.

"Empty phrases" and "many words" cannot manipulate God. Jesus did not give his disciples a set prayer to be followed word by word. Instead he taught them the way to pray in their own words as a response to God's goodness. True prayer acknowledges God as a loving parent: "Our Father." Prayer also affirms God as the supreme authority of all creation: "Our Father in heaven." Prayer accepts the hallowing (the respecting as holy) of God's name as the vocation of God's people. This respectful attitude recognizes the true nature and will of God. The person praying desires the kingdom of heaven (God's rule) as the greatest of all good. Those who pray in the proper way submit their will to the will of God because they want to be God's own agents on earth. Prayer confidently acknowledges God's goodness as the source of everything needed to sustain life. Since prayer begins by affirming God as a merciful parent, it also always requires that God's children live together mercifully, receiving and giving forgiveness of debts. Finally, prayer affirms that God will not do evil ("bring us to the time of trial") but rather God will do good ("rescue us from the evil one").

Prayer expresses vocation—the calling of a faithful people. It begins with the experience of God's extraordinary action to create an obedient people. It always ends by the people committing themselves anew to live as children of God in relationship to each other. Prayer is its own reward. It opens a person confidently to the goodness of God.

Dimension 3:
What Does the Bible Mean to Us?

If we really want to have "treasures in heaven, where neither moth nor rust consumes and where thieves do not break through and steal" (Matthew 6:20), then we will live as wise people who hear and practice what Jesus taught about almsgiving, prayer, and fasting.

The Bible material covered in this session assumes that people will be able to follow Jesus' teaching about how to give alms, pray, and fast. Jesus did not present an impossible ideal about one's relationship to God. Instead, Jesus offered a pattern of behavior that all persons were expected to accept as they were transformed from the crowds who were attracted to Jesus into disciples who followed him through the "narrow gate" and on the "hard road" that leads to life.

Practicing of Righteousness

Practicing righteousness is practicing the presence of God. Disciples live on earth as though God, who is invisible, is more important that the visible realities surrounding them. The presence of God orders the disciples' lives, because God is present with them in Jesus and in his teaching. The teaching of Jesus clarifies for his followers what their vocation is. That teaching enables them to internalize their vocation so that disciples want to do what they ought to do.

Disciples want to practice righteousness because it is the way to store up everlasting treasures in heaven (6:19-21) and it is the way to behave as children of their heavenly Father (5:43-47).

A retired man was looking forward to happy years of companionship with his wife. Then, suddenly, she became ill with Alzheimer's disease.

As the disease progressed, he found caring for her at home more and more difficult. He was forced to put her in a nursing home. He continued to visit her every day and spent as much time with her as possible. As he talked, he did not speak of the physical and emotional stress of caring for her. He did not ask for pity or for praise. Quietly, simply, straightforwardly, he told of what he did for his wife because that was what he wanted to do. When he finished describing the joy of spending a day with her in the nursing home, not sure even that she knew he was there, he asked out of the fullness of his life, "What more could any man want?"

It seems to me that he had internalized his vocation. He had stored up treasures in heaven. He was behaving like a child of his heavenly parent. His life was blessed and his life was a blessing. Although he might not have literally followed Jesus' teachings about almsgiving, prayer, and fasting, he had fulfilled all righteousness in his situation.

Righteousness of Hypocrites

Who were the people Jesus considered to be hypocrites in the Sermon on the Mount? They are described but they are not precisely identified. Perhaps the reason is that everyone is potentially a hypocrite. So, if we use Jesus' teaching about the "righteousness" of hypocrites to judge others and possibly to exclude them from our concern, then we are guilty of using Scripture to conceal our own hypocrisy.

Jesus' teachings about hypocrites calls us to repentance. They are a mirror reflecting those actions and attitudes that keep us from being faithful followers of Jesus.

Years ago when I was in theological school, I was part of a Lenten study group that read *The Screwtape Letters*, by C. S. Lewis. I still remember a sentence describing the hypocritical righteousness of a woman: "She's the sort of woman who lives for others—you can always tell the others by their hunted expression." Jesus' teaching in this lesson about the righteousness of hypocrites helps me to see now that C. S. Lewis was not writing about her; he was writing about me.

> Almsgiving, prayer, and fasting are commendable religious activities. However, if they are done self-consciously, calculatingly, and self-centeredly, they separate us from God and from our brothers and sisters.

Righteousness of Disciples

The Sermon on the Mount is not a handbook to be followed mechanically. Used in that way it becomes an end in itself rather than a means to an end, the practice of one's vocation. The almsgiving, prayer, and fasting of disciples is spontaneous, generous, and self-forgetful. Disciples do these things because they know who they are—the children of God—and because they know what they must do.

I have a friend who seems to have internalized Jesus' teaching about almsgiving, prayer, and fasting. Several years ago he was indicted for murder, sentenced to death, and imprisoned on death row. After appeal and judicial review, his conviction was reversed and he was released from prison. He had experienced the trauma of death row and the injustice of wrongful imprisonment. Yet he has not allowed his experiences to embitter him. Since his release from prison, he has devoted his time, energy, and resources to the reform of the criminal justice system in general and the abolition of the death penalty in particular. His life is an example of almsgiving because his activity on behalf of prisoners is a persistent and costly commitment to the poor. He represents what it means to pray because his communion with God is authenticated by his intercession on behalf of those who have injured society and are a threat to his own personal safety. Fasting is not something that he practices occasionally but rather the pattern of his disciplined and sacrificial devotion to doing God's will "on earth as it is in heaven." His righteousness, therefore, is not something that he practices at special times and in special places. Rather it is his vocation, which gives all of his life focus and meaning. His life is its own reward; his treasures are in heaven.

Dimension 4:
A Daily Bible Journey Plan

Day 1: Matthew 9:1-8

Day 2: Matthew 9:9-17

Day 3: Matthew 9:18-31

Day 4: Matthew 9:32-38

Day 5: Matthew 10:1-15

Day 6: Matthew 10:16-25

Day 7: Matthew 10:26-42

5

Matthew 8:1-17

The Ministry of Jesus the Messiah: Healing

What to Watch For

In this session you will study the accounts of three miraculous healings performed by Jesus according to Matthew 8:1-17. Read Matthew 8:1–9:34 to understand the background of these miracles. Watch for these key events and emphases as you read Matthew 8:1-17:

- Jesus healed a leper by touching him.
- Jesus broke the law by touching a leper but kept the law by sending him to the priest.
- Jesus healed a centurion's servant without touching him.
- Jesus would have broken the law to enter a centurion's house but he was prevented by the centurion's faith.
- Jesus healed Peter's mother-in-law by touching her.
- Peter's mother-in-law served Jesus after she was healed.
- Jesus' healing ministry fulfilled words of Isaiah.

This session will help you experience the miraculous healings of Jesus as events proclaiming the good news of the Kingdom and will help you to respond faithfully to them.

Dimension 1:
What Does the Bible Say?

1. Why did Jesus instruct the leper to say nothing to anyone, but to show himself to the priest, and offer the gift that Moses commanded as a testimony to them? (For a hint, read Leviticus 13–14.)

2. Why did the centurion prevent Jesus from coming to his house?

3. What was the quality of the centurion's faith that caused Jesus' amazement and praise?

4. What was the significance of the statement in Matthew 8:15 that Peter's mother-in-law began to serve Jesus after she was healed?

Dimension 2:
What Does the Bible Mean?

Jesus shared the good news of the Kingdom not only in his preaching and teaching but also in his healing. The stories in Matthew 8:1–9:34 about his miraculous authority over disease, nature, and demons showed how God was present to overcome all the forces threatening human life. As people experienced Jesus' power to do good, they found themselves attracted to him. However, even as the crowds expressed their amazement at Jesus' miraculous power, the Pharisees saw the same power and rejected it as evil. The Pharisees witnessed Jesus heal a person who was mute and they observed, "By the ruler of the demons he casts out the demons" (9:34).

Look up Matthew 8:1; 8:16; 9:8; and 9:33 for evidence of how Jesus' power to do good amazed and attracted people.

These stories show that Jesus did not consider himself bound by the laws concerning ritual holiness and purity found in the Hebrew Bible. Jesus willingly broke laws prohibiting contact with a leper and a sick woman. Moreover, Jesus was willing to break the law banning social contact with a Gentile. Yet as he stated in Matthew 5:17, Jesus broke the law not to abolish it but to fulfill it. He interpreted the law of Moses in the larger context of

God's promises. He therefore felt himself free to keep the law by doing what was required to fulfill those promises. He obeyed the law not by practicing it literally but by interpreting it creatively and imaginatively as God's call to serve God's people. He did not use the law to condemn people in need and to protect himself from their condition.

Instead of distancing himself from those whom the law excluded, Jesus identified with them, became unclean with them, and included them in his mercy. This radical action arose from his sense of vocation and his commitment to live according to God's will. Jesus fulfilled what the prophet Isaiah had spoken, "He took our infirmities and bore our diseases" (Matthew 8:17; Isaiah 53:4).

> Jesus fulfilled what the prophet Isaiah had spoken, "He took our infirmities and bore our diseases."

Healing as Restoration to Community

The term *leprosy* as used in the Bible referred to any skin disease causing swelling, eruptions, boils, spots, rashes, or abnormal loss of hair. Hebrew law and society considered persons afflicted with leprosy to be ritually unclean for leprosy prevented a person from participating in the worship of God. A person cured of leprosy had to undergo a complicated purification procedure over a period of many days before being pronounced clean by the priest. Persons and objects touched by a leper became themselves ritually unclean. They, too, were forced to undergo an elaborate cleansing process. Garments or other objects considered unclean were burned.

These laws originally arose from the belief that Israel was a holy people, devoted to God and separated from sin. The laws of cleanliness reminded Israel of its special relationship to God and were intended to keep the nation pure for the service of God. The prophets interpreted holiness differently, however, and called upon the people to purify themselves not by external rituals but by internal repentance. They called for a purity of heart expressed in acts of mercy and justice (Isaiah 1:16; Ezekiel 36:25).

The story in Matthew 8:1-4 shows how Jesus broke down the barriers of clean and unclean that separated and excluded some from the community. A leper had heard about Jesus' ministry. In spite of the laws declaring him unfit for contact with clean persons, the leper still approached Jesus. Instead of doing what the law required of him (remaining outside the community and warning others to avoid him by crying out, "Unclean, unclean"), the leper approached Jesus. He took the initiative to get Jesus to help him. He knelt before Jesus with a worshipful attitude. He acknowledged Jesus' authority by calling him "Lord." His request affirmed Jesus' power. He awaited Jesus' decision. This man never doubted that Jesus could make him clean. He only wondered whether Jesus would *choose* to make him clean.

Jesus responded immediately. Jesus did not question the man about his past. Nor did he tell the man to do anything that he had not already done. "He stretched out his hand and touched him" (8:3). The touch that ritually defiled Jesus was the condition for the cleansing. The leper could doubt no longer. Jesus chose to do what was good for the leper without qualification, without condition, without hesitation. He was the leper's Emmanuel because he chose to fulfill all righteousness not by doing what "was said to those of ancient times" (5:23, 33) but by reinterpreting the law as God's inclusive love for all people. Jesus broke the laws of clean and unclean, showing how the laws could be fulfilled by acts of mercy.

The central emphasis of the story is not that Jesus had the power to cleanse the leper but that Jesus restored the leper to the community. Jesus' touching him was a dramatic breaking down of the wall of clean and unclean that excluded the leper. However, restoration to the community could not take place until the cure had been acknowledged by the priest and the prescribed ritual performed. Jesus broke the law by touching the leper (Leviticus 5:3) and then commanded the leper to fulfill the law by saying nothing about the healing until the priest's acknowledgment and the leper's gift ritually confirmed it.

Healing as Enlargement of Community

These stories of healing shift us away from the region near the setting for the Sermon on the Mount and back to Capernaum. The cosmopolitan population of Capernaum included Gentiles. Probably the gracious outreach of Jesus' house welcomed Gentiles. Remember the claim made in Matthew 4:12-16 that Jesus was the "light" to the Gentiles prophesied by Isaiah. We should not be surprised that a prominent Gentile, a Roman centurion, came to Jesus, appealing for help on behalf of his servant.

Jesus' vocation was to be "the light of the world." His lamp had been put on the lampstand so that it gave "light to all in the house" (5:14-15), even to a Roman military officer considered an enemy of the Jewish people. Jesus' good works, including his healing ministry, were not limited to the circle of his "brothers and sisters." They included his "enemies" and those "who persecuted" him (5:43-48).

Jesus affirmed the centurion's action as a model for response to the good news of the Kingdom. The centurion addressed Jesus as "Lord," acknowledging that Jesus held the authority of God. He not only said, "Lord, Lord," but he also acted in a way consistent with Jesus' teachings (7:21).

The centurion humbled himself and became an advocate for a person who had no power, his servant. Moreover, he expressed an unwavering confidence in the power of Jesus to do good. All of this behavior was so unusual, so exemplary, that Jesus turned to his followers and said to them, "Truly I tell you, in no one in Israel have I found such faith. I tell you many will come from east and west and will eat with Abraham and Isaac and Jacob in the kingdom of heaven, while the heirs of the kingdom will be thrown into the outer darkness, where there will be weeping and gnashing of teeth" (8:10-12).

The centurion embodied what Jesus wanted from his followers: faith. Faith was made possible by the good news of the Kingdom but it was not coerced. The centurion chose to trust Jesus' power to do what was needed. His place in the kingdom of heaven was assured not by his racial, religious, political, or social background, but by the fact that he had learned to treasure what was ultimately important. Those who failed to meet the test of the centurion's faith would be excluded from the kingdom of heaven. If they traced their physical descent to Abraham and obeyed the law meticulously but failed to practice mercy, they would still not enter the kingdom of heaven. Jesus praised the centurion because he represented the universal extension of the community of faith to include "many from east and west."

The healing of the centurion's servant seems almost incidental in this story. The centurion's compassion had already provided the context in which the cure was possible. His unwavering confidence in the inclusive goodness of Jesus and his self-giving concern for his servant created a community in which God's will was "done on earth as it is in heaven" (6:10). The centurion's prayer for his servant's cure was not necessary to instruct or manipulate God (6:25-34). It was necessary for the fulfillment of the centurion's vocation, for his becoming an agent through whom God's goodness was realized in the miraculous healing of his servant. The centurion had obeyed the gospel and had learned what the Scriptures taught, "I desire mercy, not sacrifice" (Matthew 9:13; Hosea, 6:6).

Healing as Qualification for Ministry

The story about the healing of Peter's mother-in-law expands the themes introduced in the healings of the leper and the centurion's servant. Just as Jesus became unclean when "he stretched out his hand and touched" the leper, so he likewise became unclean when "he touched" the hand of Peter's mother-in-law.

However, not only was Peter's mother-in-law raised up from her bed and delivered from her fever, she also "began to serve him." The words *to serve* translated in the New Revised Standard Version of the Bible come from the Greek word *diakonei* from which the English words *deacon* and *ministry* come. The woman's healing was her call to her vocation. Jesus sought her out in her condition of need, restored her to the community, and equipped her to do the work of the community.

Matthew used this story to remind the church at Antioch that *all* disciples of Jesus were created by the ministry of Jesus. *All* were unclean until they were healed by the Physician. *All* were sinners until they were called to the righteousness of ministry. *All* were qualified for ministry not by their accomplishments, not by their knowledge, not by their purity, but by the grace of God.

Dimension 3: What Does the Bible Mean to Us?

Matthew reported these accounts of the healing ministry of Jesus not as special instances of Jesus' authority but as typical examples of how disciples respond to the good news of the kingdom of heaven. References to discipleship run throughout Matthew 8:1–9:34. Disciples leave their homes, their families, their "nests," their "holes" to follow Jesus (8:18-22). Their sickness has been healed by the Physician (9:12). They have been called from sin to the righteousness of following Jesus (9:13). Therefore, the stories about Jesus' miraculous healings are intended to help disciples understand who they are and what they ought to be doing.

Healing as Restoration to Community

Who are the lepers in our society today? Who are the unclean?

Did you come up with a list of persons or types of people in response to these questions? However, if the story tells about how Jesus included *all* persons in his community and called *all* persons to the work of the community, then the story is not about other persons but about *us*.

We tend to divide the human family into two groups, clean and unclean, well and sick, righteous and sinners. Jesus' ministry calls this division into question. Jesus did not recognize such distinctions. He treated all persons as if they were unclean, sick, and sinners.

The only thing that can shut us out of the kingdom of heaven is the presumption on our part that *we* are clean, well, righteous. Only those who know they are unclean can be made clean. Only those who know they are sick can be cured. Only those who know they are sinners can be called to righteousness. We reveal that we know our condition when we respond to the miraculous power of Jesus by saying with the crowds, "Never has anything like this been seen in Israel." We reveal our ignorance of our condition by saying with the Pharisees, "By the ruler of the demons he casts out the demons."

Healing as Enlargement of Community

We continue to live in exclusive communities. We think the enlargement of community is optional and up to our choice. The story about the healing of the centurion's servant presents an entirely different understanding. Jesus' commendation to the centurion leaves no room for doubt. Those who continue to live in exclusive communities, regardless of their ethnic, cultural, or religious ancestry, will themselves be excluded from the kingdom of heaven.

> The Pharisees asked Jesus' disciples, "Why does your teacher eat with tax collectors and sinners?" (11). Look up Jesus' response in Matthew 9:12. His answer undermines the presupposition of the question.

The application to our contemporary situation is crystal clear. An exclusive house is not the Jesus house. An institution that reflects distinctions between clean and unclean, well and sick, righteous and sinners is not an agency of the kingdom of heaven. A segregated church, whether segregation happens intentionally or unintentionally, is not a community of disciples.

What then is the good news? God calls us to an absolutely inclusive community and still maintains God's presence with us in our exclusive brokenness. God creates wholeness by the gift of inclusive love.

We may settle for something less than the perfection of God's love that includes us all. But God makes no compromises. God continues to love us without regard for our condition. God showers blessings upon us even when we have chosen to rebel against God's will for our lives.

We continue to experience "weeping and gnashing of teeth" in a racist and divided society. As painful as that fact is, it is a sign that God's news claims us for something better than hatred and hostility. God's desire to include all God's children is so powerful and so persistent that we can never live happily ever after in broken and divided communities.

The choice is always ours but the consequences of our choices are inevitable. We will either join many who come from east and west to "eat with Abraham and Isaac and Jacob in the kingdom of heaven," or we "will be thrown into outer darkness, where there will be weeping and gnashing of teeth."

Healing as Qualification for Ministry

Jesus' healing restores persons to community and enlarges that community so that all persons are included. Jesus is able to heal because he gives himself without limit to the fulfillment of all righteousness, or his vocation. Those who are healed by him are qualified by his self-giving love to join him in fulfilling their vocation. Disciples of Jesus are

> God calls us to an absolutely inclusive community and still maintains God's presence with us in our exclusive brokenness. God creates wholeness by the gift of inclusive love.

those who have been healed by his ministry and who take upon themselves the ministry of healing.

I have a friend whose life has helped me to see how we are all recipients of the healing ministry of Jesus as well as agents of that ministry. My friend is a recovering alcoholic. He understands himself as a weak and vulnerable person who is able to stay sober because he is surrounded by the love of God offered to him through his family and friends. They have not judged him harshly nor excluded him from their lives. Rather they have taken upon themselves his infirmity and his disease. His recovery process has restored him to community and helped him to experience the fact that there is no healing without a community of mercy.

In his weakness and vulnerability he has discovered power and security. He has been able to be with other persons in their struggles to overcome drug and alcohol addiction. He now understands himself as a disciple by the grace of God's healing ministry in Jesus. The ministry that reached out to him and touched him in his uncleanness has made him clean and raised him up to reach out and include others in his service of love. Although he experienced the good news of the Kingdom as personal healing, it was a healing that overcame the isolation of his disease and incorporated him in a community of compassion. The healing he now offers to others is the natural result of his own experience of healing. The promise of Jesus to Peter and Andrew, "Follow me, and I will make you fish for people," has been fulfilled in his life as he has given freely what he freely received (4:18-19).

Dimension 4:
A Daily Bible Journey Plan

Day 1: Matthew 11:1-9

Day 2: Matthew 11:20-30

Day 3: Matthew 12:1-14

Day 4: Matthew 12:15-32

Day 5: Matthew 12:33-42

Day 6: Matthew 12:43-50

Day 7: Matthew 13:1-9

Matthew 9:35–10:25

6 THE MINISTRY OF JESUS THE MESSIAH ACCEPTED: AUTHORITY TO PREACH AND HEAL

What to Watch For

This session looks at Matthew 9:35–10:25. This passage is part of a larger section that continues through Matthew 13:53. Matthew arranged this material to help followers understand their vocation, the rejection encountered by them in their vocation, and the way rejection resulted in mission to the Gentiles.

- Jesus' ministry included "teaching in their synagogues, and proclaiming the good news of the Kingdom, and curing every disease and every sickness" (9:35).
- Jesus gave his twelve disciples authority "over unclean spirits, to cast them out, and to cure every disease and every sickness" (10:1).
- The Twelve were sent "to the lost sheep of the house of Israel" (10:6).
- The Twelve would be supported in their mission by the goodness of God.
- The mission of the Twelve would be peace to the house that is "worthy" but judgment to the house "not worthy" (10:12-13).
- The Twelve would be rejected by Israel.
- Rejection by Israel would result in testimony to Gentiles.
- Hatred endured would result in salvation.
- Persecution would enlarge the mission.
- Rejection of the Twelve would be similar to the rejection of Jesus.

This session seeks to help those who follow Jesus accept their vocation, persevere in their vocation, and become like Jesus in their vocation.

43

Dimension 1: What Does the Bible Say?

1. Why were the crowds in Israel "harassed and helpless, like sheep without a shepherd"? *Lost*

2. What does the word *harvest* mean? Who is "the Lord" of the harvest? *people* — *God*

3. What makes the house "worthy" or "not worthy"? *receptive to message*

4. Why is it "enough for the disciple to be like the teacher, and the slave like the master" (10:25)?

Dimension 2: What Does the Bible Mean?

Matthew used these texts to instruct the church at Antioch. These texts consist of the traditions Matthew had received about how Jesus gathered his disciples and prepared them to participate in his ministry. For Matthew, Jesus' teaching about the nature and work of the people of God offered the most important resource for the church in Antioch as it faced the challenge of a hostile Jewish community and an unfriendly Gentile environment. If the church remembered what it was, then the church would know what to do.

Jesus' Vocation: Reformation of the People of God

As you recall from the angel's visit to Joseph, Jesus' vocation had been from the beginning to "save his people from their sins" (1:21). The people sinned because they had forgotten that God had chosen them not for privilege but for ministry. Losing sight of their task to bring God's blessing to all nations, they sought to appease God by sacrifices instead of becoming like God in mercy. Thereby, they lost their blessing. Within this context, Jesus came preaching and teaching the good news of the Kingdom so that his people would repent.

Repentance meant centering one's life in God as the greatest possible good.

Jesus also practiced the good news of the Kingdom by "curing every disease and every sickness" (9:35). By giving up his own power and authority, Jesus became the agent of God's authority and became able to carry out his ministry of healing. By identifying the needs of people and giving his life in ministry, Jesus was not so much the judge of the last days but the revealer of God's merciful reign on earth.

Jesus did not condemn those in the crowd who were "harassed and helpless" (9:36). Instead he enlisted his disciples to serve as agents of divine compassion. The greatest need of the "harassed and helpless" crowds of Israel was that they were "like sheep without a shepherd"—that is, they did not know God as their king whose authority was expressed in unfailing love. In their exposure to the ministry of Jesus, the disciples had already, to some extent, recognized God's authority or reign and had chosen it as the treasure of their lives. That choice made them candidates to join Jesus in his ministry of compassion.

But not even Jesus could make his disciples do anything that they did not want to do. All that Jesus could do was call their attention to the opportunity for service. Jesus now expected the disciples to do what Israel had failed to do. Just as Jesus had claimed his own vocation by depending upon God's word, so the disciples were instructed by Jesus to claim their own vocation by obeying Jesus' word (4:1-11; 5:13-16). They should first respond by praying to "the Lord of the harvest to send out laborers into his harvest" (9:38).

> "The harvest is plentiful, but the laborers are few" (9:37). Often the association of the word *harvest* with the Last Judgment gave it a negative meaning. In this context, however, it is a metaphor for the consummation of God's saving purpose for the world. Here it has an overwhelmingly positive meaning. In this passage Jesus used *harvest* to speak figuratively of the fulfillment of God's gracious promises and to underscore the fact that God uses faithful followers as agents of salvation. This text implies that God had called Israel to be "laborers" in the "harvest" for the sake of the world.

Prayer focused the disciples' attention upon God and God's will. Prayer also helped the disciples clarify that they wanted the kingdom of heaven more than anything else. Only those who were single-minded in their devotion to God were qualified for hallowing God's name and doing God's will "on earth as it is in heaven" (6:9-10, 22-24).

Jesus' vocation required the summoning and equipping of "the twelve disciples" for ministry. Matthew 10:2-4 provides the first listing of twelve disciples or apostles, designating the inner core of Jesus' followers. Matthew's first readers immediately associated the number *twelve* with the twelve tribes of Israel. They understood that "the twelve" did not merely refer to twelve individuals but to the whole people of God, renewed and recommissioned for God's service.

> The apostles were not puppets on a string but people choosing what they wanted to do.

Those first readers were themselves summoned and equipped by Jesus with the authority of self-giving love to attack all the forces of evil that threatened human life. Those who prayed that they would be sent out as laborers into God's harvest were now called "apostles," that is those sent by God to do God's work. They were not puppets on a string but people choosing what they wanted to do. If they failed to choose God's will, they would destroy themselves. God's summoning and choosing always includes the possibility of "Judas Iscariot, the one who betrayed him."

The Vocation of the Reformed People of God

The salvation of the Gentiles was the ultimate objective of God's creation of a people. When the people forgot their identity and mission, then God's concern was their reformation. Therefore Jesus sent the Twelve, the reformed people of God, to call the entire people to repentance so that they might enjoy the blessing of the kingdom of heaven (5:1-11). The message that had transformed their lives was now to be their message "to the lost sheep of the house of Israel." The model for their ministry was the ministry that they had received from Jesus. Since he was present with them as their Emmanuel, they could "go, proclaim the good news, 'The kingdom of heaven has come near.' Cure the sick, raise the dead, cleanse the lepers, cast out demons" (10:7-8).

The Twelve were sent to give what they had received. Their ministry was rooted and grounded in the goodness of God. They depended upon that goodness and left everything else: gold, silver, copper, bag, tunics, sandals, and staff. They trusted the good news they shared to provide the hospitality they needed.

They were not responsible for their reception but only for the integrity of their message and service. Their words and deeds would become either blessing or judgment depending upon whether they were received or rejected. Their peace would rest upon houses that were worthy, that is, those households that received them. The good news of the Kingdom would become bad news on the Day of Judgment for all who refused to repent and believe in the gospel. If rejected by people who would not acknowledge the reign of God, they were to leave them by shaking off the dust from their feet—the traditional action of a righteous Jew leaving unholy ground.

The Reformed People of God and the Gentile Mission

In Matthew 10:16, Jesus used the images of sheep, wolves, serpents, and doves. "Sheep" knew their king and went into the harvest as servants of their king. Those to whom they were sent, "wolves," had become evil because they did not know their king and served themselves. Jesus sent his disciples to assault evil with the good news of the Kingdom. They were instructed to "be wise as serpents and innocent as doves." Their wisdom was in their fear of God rather than of human authorities (10:26-33). Their resistance to evil by doing good to those who reviled and persecuted them demonstrated their innocence (5:10-12, 38-42).

The disciples would be rejected by "the lost sheep of the house of Israel." But rejection by the house of Israel would become the occasion for mission to the Gentiles. Just as God intervened miraculously in the history of Israel to maintain a people of God not dependent upon physical descent from Abraham (1:3, 5, 6, 18, 20), so God fulfilled the promise of salvation for the Gentiles by using the rejection of the gospel to spread the gospel. The Twelve, representing the reformed people of God, would be handed over to councils, flogged in synagogues, and dragged before governors and kings; but they would not be overcome. They would witness to the kingdom of heaven by their wisdom and innocence. The inclusion of the Gentiles enlarged the scope of their ministry, but it never excluded Israel and was possible because the Twelve had heard and obeyed the gospel and represented the reformed people of God, the new Israel.

> The Twelve, representing the reformed people of God, would be handed over to councils, flogged in synagogues, and dragged before governors and kings; but they would not be overcome.

Jesus referred to the persecution of the Twelve as a "testimony" or witness. The Greek word is *marturion*, which is the root of our English word *martyr*. The Twelve witnessed not so much by what they said but by who they were. Being witnesses was more important than bearing witness. Their lives authenticated their words. Therefore they were not to worry about their words of testimony any more than they were to worry about their lives. They were sustained and empowered by the Spirit. Anxiety for their message or for their life would discredit their testimony. It would reveal that they feared human authority more than the authority of God, that they trusted their own power rather than the power of God.

As representatives of the reformed people of God, the Twelve shifted their allegiance from their human families to the household of God. They faced the hatred of all who still clung to security of the old order, including the hatred of family members. Salvation came by enduring the hatred of all and by loving their enemies (5:43-44; 10:34-39).

The disciples found their greatest reward in what they became by the grace of God, not in anything they might have received. They shared a vocation with Jesus. Just as Jesus had humbled himself and identified with the needs of God's children, so they were clearly identified as his disciples by being like him in humble service. That was enough. Their reward was revilement and persecution just as Jesus was reviled and persecuted. Their lives interpreted the meaning of the beatitude: "Blessed are those who are persecuted for righteousness' sake, for theirs is the kingdom of heaven" (5:10). They were God's faithful witnesses not merely because of their words but because they had lost their lives for the sake of Jesus and had found it (10:38-39). They were saved because they had a vocation, a purpose, a calling.

Dimension 3:
What Does the Bible Mean to Us?

These texts remind us that God has created the church—the reformed people of God—not for the sake of the church but for the sake of the world. They also help us to see that God guides, comforts, and strengthens the church as it responds to God's call to humble service. These texts call the church to repentance by instructing the church that salvation from sin always involves choosing to be agents of God's harvest.

Jesus' Vocation:
Reformation of the People of God

The church sometimes tends to forget who has ultimate authority, who is in charge. Our greatest resource as a people of God, however, is that Jesus is present with us as one whose compassion does not fail. In our harassed and helpless condition, his self-giving love directs our attention to God and reveals God as the provider of all that we need to fulfill our lives.

The traditions about Jesus' ministry report what Jesus did during his earthly ministry. They also enable us to experience what Jesus continues to do in the church as the crucified and risen Lord of the church.

I recently heard of the way an affluent, suburban church was called to repentance by the life and ministry of Jesus. This church voted to take $40,000 from its endowment to make available low interest loans to provide housing for poor people. The church also secured a matching $40,000 grant from a church agency to increase the total available to $80,000.

This response to a specific need was an answer to prayer. The church saw the plentiful harvest and the few laborers. It prayed for "the Lord of the harvest to send out laborers into his harvest." God answered its prayer by commissioning and equipping it for this mission. The church is always more than an institution. It is the creation of One who calls his followers, gives them authority to join him in his work, and sends them as "laborers into the harvest."

The Vocation of the Reformed People of God

Our task as the reformed people of God is to carry on a "lover's quarrel with the church." This means that our calling to be what God intends for us to be is always in tension with what we actually are. We make a mistake when we identify too quickly and too easily with the apostles instead of with "the lost sheep of the house of Israel." How often we become defensive and self-serving when we are confronted by those faithful messengers whom God has sent to call us to repentance and to save us from our sins! Our reflex action is to silence them by saying, "That's not the way we do it here," or by accusing them of being agents of evil. Our reception of God's messengers is not a trivial matter. As these texts make clear, how we welcome and listen to those who have left everything to proclaim the good news of the kingdom of heaven will determine our ultimate destiny.

> Our task as the reformed people of God is to carry on a "lover's quarrel with the church."

Among the clearest apostolic voices we hear today comes from those who renounce war as an acceptable means for settling international disputes. But instead of welcoming them and listening to their words, we silence them by dismissing them as idle dreamers. Or we attack them as unpatriotic enemies of our country. Those who dared raise their voices in criticism of our nation's engagement in the Gulf War encountered personal attacks and ridicule not only from the government but also from within the Christian community.

Our problem is not that God has stopped sending out messengers to "the lost sheep of the house of Israel," but rather that we, in our complacency and self-righteousness, have sometimes refused to welcome them or to listen to their words. The warning of the text is clear: When we reject the messengers of peace, we reveal that we have rejected peace itself.

The Reformed People of God and the Gentile Mission

These texts, although realistic about the resistance that the good news encounters, are the ground of triumphant hope. They help us to experience the fact that God's yes to the world can never be silenced by the no of the world. God's promise to bless the Gentiles through a people chosen to be agents of service, rather than recipients of privilege, cannot be thwarted. God does not falter in purpose nor waver in mercy. Therefore, God's intervention transformed the rejection of the apostolic messengers and the apostolic message.

Neither are those sent by God today defeated by the opposition they often receive within the Christian community. Because they fear God rather than human authorities and depend upon the power of God's love rather than violence, their witness is made not only in the church but throughout the world. Like the apostles of old they are a testimony to "the lost sheep of the house of Israel" and to "the Gentiles."

Persecution of so-called heretics is one of the facts of church history. But some within the church have always denounced the use of violence to silence dissent. Although torture still occurs, neither the church nor the world condones or defends it as a legitimate expression of authority. Thus the witness of the martyrs has prevailed.

Likewise, for centuries the church either tolerated or condoned the institution of slavery. Yet the good news has always proclaimed release of slaves. The movement for the abolition of modern slavery originated within the church. Today slavery is universally condemned not only by the church but by the world. So it is clear that the apostolic witness, in spite of opposition within the Christian community, has prevailed not only among "the lost sheep of the house of Israel" but also among "the Gentiles."

These texts challenge us to risk identifying the apostolic witnesses whose rejection today has enlarged the scope of the apostolic mission. We hear the words of apostolic witnesses in the voices of those who speak out for the rights of women. We know that they have been condemned and discredited within the Christian community by those who quote Scripture and appeal to tradition to keep women in subservient roles in the church and society. Nevertheless, the liberating message of the good news for women has never been silenced. The apostolic witness has established women as leaders in many branches of the Christian church and has been a powerful force for justice and equality for women in politics, business, and society generally. Much still remains to be accomplished, especially in societies where hierarchical traditions of male supremacy still deny women justice and equality. These texts encourage us to believe that violent resistance to the cause of women only serves to spread the word and assure its eventual victory.

Dimension 4:
A Daily Bible Journey Plan

Day 1: Matthew 13:10-23

Day 2: Matthew 13:24-32

Day 3: Matthew 13:33-43

Day 4: Matthew 13:44-58

Day 5: Matthew 14:1-12

Day 6: Matthew 14:13-21

Day 7: Matthew 14:22-36

Matthew 12:22-37

7

THE MINISTRY OF JESUS THE MESSIAH REJECTED: BLASPHEMY AGAINST THE HOLY SPIRIT

What to Watch For

Read Matthew 12:22-37 for this session. The text draws sharply the conflict between Jesus and those who clung to the security and power of the old order. The seriousness of this conflict is clearly stated in 12:22-37 as Jesus responded to the charge that he was able to overcome evil because he himself was an agent of evil power.

- The conflict started when Jesus cured "a demoniac who was blind and mute" (22).
- The crowds were amazed and responded positively to the miraculous cure (23).
- The Pharisees sought to discredit Jesus' ministry by accusing him of casting out demons "by Beelzebul, the ruler of the demons" (24).

> See such passages as Matthew 9:34; 10:4, 16-25, 34-39; 12:14 for other indications.

- Jesus countered their accusation by showing the absurdity of saying evil forces brought victory over evil. He reminded them that such logic would require them to reject their own exorcists (27).
- Blasphemy against the power of the kingdom of God was blasphemy against the Holy Spirit and would not be forgiven (31).
- What people said about Jesus' ministry would be the basis of their fate on the Day of Judgment. Their words about his deeds revealed the allegiance of their hearts (37).

In this session you will experience the ministry of Jesus as a call to repentance that, when rejected, excludes one from the forgiveness God always offers.

Dimension 1:
What Does the Bible Say?

1. Why did Jesus' healing of the man who was blind and mute because of demons lead the crowds to wonder whether Jesus might be "the Son of David"? (What is the significance of the phrase, *the Son of David?*) *Messiah*

2. What motivated the Pharisees to accuse Jesus of casting out demons "by Beelzebul, the ruler of the demons"?
To discredit Jesus driving out demons

3. Why did Jesus declare that rejection of his ministry was blasphemy against the Holy Spirit, which would not be forgiven?
deliberately & intentionally using derogatory language against God

4. What did Jesus mean when he said, "For out of the abundance of the heart the mouth speaks" (34)?
The mouth speaks what is truly in the heart

Dimension 2:
What Does the Bible Mean?

Matthew understood the ministry of Jesus as a manifestation of the kingdom of heaven or the kingdom of God. The deeds of Jesus, his "curing every disease and every sickness" (4:23) embodied what he preached: "the good news of the kingdom" (9:35). Therefore, one needed to keep in mind Jesus' message of repentance in order to understand and receive what he did.

In this text the kingdom of God came both to the crowds and to the Pharisees when "a demoniac who was blind and mute" was brought to Jesus. Jesus "cured him, so that the one who had been mute could speak and see" (12:22). In this way Jesus revealed "the good news of the kingdom" in his healing ministry. People properly responded when they turned from the security and power of the old order and put their trust in the security and power of God's gracious presence.

Jesus' Ministry: Call to Repentance

Matthew used this passage to remind the church at Antioch that people who were in need—suffering from demon possession, infirmities, and diseases—were the recipients of the mercy of God. They were neither condemned nor excluded because of their condition. When they were brought to Jesus, they were cured. The healing revealed the good news: God was with them in their need to deliver them from everything that kept them from living as God's children.

Jesus made God's will his will through his obedient relationship to God. He revealed God's goodness in his words and deeds. God's will is not a heavy burden, because God's mercy draws people to him and makes them want to be like him. Those who were drawn to Jesus became like him by depending upon God's mercy and by being merciful to each other. The power of God's goodness turned them away from the false teaching about God, the hard yoke of special privilege and self-righteousness. And it turned them to the truth about God, the easy yoke of vocation and the light burden of gentleness and humility.

Matthew wanted the church at Antioch to experience anew God's call to repentance. The church did not possess the good news of the Kingdom automatically. The good news had to be claimed freely and wholeheartedly in light of the changing situation of the church and the new demands of God's mercy. If the church did not hear and see the gospel as God's call to repentance, then the good news of the Kingdom would become the bad news of God's judgment. The choice was sharply drawn by the words and deeds of Jesus: "Whoever is not with me is against me, and whoever does not gather with me scatters" (12:30).

> **Repentance** - A complete reorientation of one's life involving a negative judgment of the past and a deliberate redirection for the future. The prophetic call for repentance was a summons from a complete turnabout that was to arise from the heart, the seat of the will. John echoed the prophetic message in his preaching. This call was central to the proclamation of Jesus.

Jesus' Ministry: Final Judgment

Matthew presented the ministry of Jesus as a vocation Jesus was able to carry out because he had been given the power of God—the Holy Spirit. Jesus' works were not his own works but the works of the Spirit of God.

Because Jesus' acts of mercy called all people to join him in a ministry of mercy (9:9-13), those persons who thought they had a place of special privilege with God felt threatened by Jesus' ministry. Instead of joining the crowds in amazement and speculation about the possibility that Jesus was the Messiah, the Son of David, the Pharisees sought to discredit Jesus and thereby maintain their own positions of power and authority.

These Pharisees not only represented those Jews who rejected the ministry of Jesus, they also represented an attitude that had developed within

> **Holy Spirit** - The power of God operative in creation, salvation, and consummation. In the Hebrew Scriptures the Holy Spirit or Spirit of God is often given to persons to empower them for a specific task. In the New Testament Jesus is empowered by the Holy Spirit for his ministry. Jesus assumed that the Holy Spirit was also active among his followers, giving them the authority or power to preach, teach, and heal.

the church itself. The Spirit of God continued to empower the ministry of the church after the death and resurrection of Jesus. Some within the church, however (especially some leaders), felt threatened by an inclusive ministry. In order to maintain their own base of power, they condemned the liberating and inclusive ministry of the Holy Spirit. Those who rejected the ministry of the Holy Spirit could not, of course, threaten the power of the Holy Spirit. However, those persons excluded themselves from the kingdom of God and brought themselves under the judgment of God.

The Pharisees said, "It is only by Beelzebul, the ruler of the demons, that this fellow casts out the demons" (24). Jesus responded not so much to defend himself as to proclaim the decisive nature of his ministry. His ministry was an assault upon all forms of evil, because he was the agent of the Spirit of God who entered the strong man's house, tied him up, and plundered his property. What was said about his own Spirit-empowered ministry was also true of the Spirit-empowered ministry of the church. Jesus' merciful and inclusive ministry continued in the words and deeds of his faithful followers. To resist or to hinder that ministry was to be an enemy of God and an ally of evil. No one can be neutral in the presence of the good news of the Kingdom. "Whoever is not with me is against me, and whoever does not gather with me scatters" (12:30).

Jesus' Ministry: Radical Change

Jesus' ministry sought to bring about transformation in the lives of people. His vocation was to "make the tree good, and its fruit good" (12:33); to create "good persons" who brought "good things out of a good treasure"; to enable people to "speak good things" from the "abundance" of their hearts.

> **Beelzebul** - [bee-el'zi-buhl] In the New Testament a name given to the chief of demons (Satan). The Pharisees applied it to Jesus to discredit his healing of the demon-possessed.

People become what they desire, what they treasure. If people give their hearts, their innermost being, over to evil, then they will be bad; their deeds will be bad; their speech will be evil. On the other hand, if they give their hearts over to good, then they will be good; their deeds will be good; their speech will be good.

How did Jesus undertake to accomplish his vocation? He did not coerce or manipulate people. He showed them the kingdom of God by showing them the mercy of God. He invited all persons to come to

THE UNFORGIVABLE SIN: BLASPHEMY AGAINST THE HOLY SPIRIT

Jesus labeled this Pharisaic attitude as "blasphemy against the Spirit." Technically, blasphemy was the sin of deliberately and intentionally using derogatory language about God. Old Testament laws called for blasphemy to be punished by stoning (Leviticus 24:16). In this lesson Jesus warned that speaking against the Holy Spirit mocked God and was therefore more serious than a personal attack on Jesus. He underscored the dreadful seriousness of reviling God's power by stating that it would "not be forgiven, either in this age or in the age to come." God does not withdraw forgiveness in this case; but so long as one did not recognize one's need and receive the forgiveness freely offered, not even God could give the mercy a person rejected.

To reject God's mercy meant deciding to shut God out of one's life and to live on the basis of one's own security and power. This difficult text seeks to help people perceive the horrible, ultimate consequences of rejecting the merciful ministry of Jesus. The harsh saying was merciful because it called people to turn from their own self-righteousness and turn to the one who was "gentle and humble in heart" and find rest for their souls.

him. He delivered them from the evil that blinded them to the mercy of God and that kept them from speaking for the mercy of God. Jesus was confident that when people saw the mercy of God, they would desire God above all else. They would reveal the good treasure of their heart in their words and deeds.

Jesus' own words and deeds arose from the abundance of his heart, from his complete dedication to the will of God. He was a good person who out of his good treasure brought forth good things. Since he was a good tree, his fruit was good. He wanted others to become what he was; and he sought to make them want to be as he was by being faithful to his heart's allegiance. He authenticated his invitation by what he said and did: "Come to me, all you that are weary and are carrying heavy burdens, and I will give you rest. Take my yoke upon you, and learn from me; for I am gentle and humble in heart, and you will find rest for your souls. For my yoke is easy, and my burden is light" (11:28-30).

When persons rejected the ministry of Jesus, he was not vindictive or hateful. Neither was he passive or indifferent to the words of persons whose words about him were evil because they treasured their own privilege and trusted their own power. He sought to change the misdirection of their lives by warning them that their evil "treasure" would make them evil. They would condemn themselves by what they had become. The Last Judgment had already come for them because by their words they would be condemned. But it was not too late for them. If they would come to him in their need and claim what he offered, they could yet become faithful followers.

Dimension 3: What Does the Bible Mean to Us?

This lesson helps us reflect on how we relate ourselves to the ministry of Jesus. Jesus' ministry as related in the Book of Matthew is more than an event that happened in the distant past. Rather it is a continuing work of the Holy Spirit among the faithful followers of Jesus today.

This text focuses our attention upon the fact that the kingdom of God has come to us in acts of mercy that reveal the nature of God. We cannot remain neutral in the presence of the good news of the Kingdom. Our response reveals the allegiance of our hearts. Jesus said: "Whoever is not with me is against me, and whoever does not gather with me scatters" (12:30).

Jesus' Ministry: Call to Repentance

The word *repent* does not occur in this text, yet it is this response that the text intends to inspire in us. All that Jesus has said and done through the Holy Spirit is a revelation of the mercy of God. God is with us not as a tyrant or a vindictive judge but as a loving parent. This means that each time the merciful ministry of the Holy Spirit enables us to see God clearly, we find ourselves confronted with the difference between our ways and the ways of God.

The details of this experience may change, but the basic reality remains fundamentally the same. No matter what our condition, we always come to the ministry of God's mercy as persons who must be healed like the person whom Jesus healed in this passage. Being healed will enable us to see the truth about God and speak the truth of God's mercy. We know that we are in the presence of God's Spirit when we hear the preaching of Jesus as a summons to change our lives. "Repent, for the kingdom of heaven has come near" (4:17).

> God is with us not as a tyrant or a vindictive judge but as a loving parent.

A friend and I had a serious discussion about how we should relate to persons whose lifestyle is different from our own and, from our perspective, seems to be wrong. We had prior assumptions and values; yet we desired to be more open and affirming of persons whom we had been conditioned to exclude and condemn.

The discussion was painful and exhausting. It was painful because we were being pushed by our dialogue to acknowledge that we had only begun to learn what it means to desire mercy more than sacrifice. It was exhausting because we were dealing with the enemy of prejudice and fear in our own hearts. I am convinced that we experienced anew the power of the Holy Spirit calling us to repent, to give our allegiance to God's mercy.

Jesus' Ministry: Final Judgment

You may be familiar with speculation about "the unforgivable sin." You might have heard of people who have punished themselves cruelly by concluding that they have done something God cannot forgive. Such conclusions are wrong. These people abuse this text because they assume that God's mercy is limited by the horrible fact of some human transgression.

The Bible text affirms the opposite. God's mercy is infinite. However, only those who freely accept it can receive it. God reveals the infinite quality of God's mercy by God's waiting in this age and in the age to come for people to accept what is always offered.

The Pharisaic attitude toward God is not limited to an ancient Jewish sect. It is present in all religions. It often manifests itself in our own behavior. An analogy from our common experience may help to clarify this point.

Suppose a husband and wife have lived together happily for a long time. Then the husband violates his marriage vows and hides his unfaithfulness from his wife. He assumes that since no one knows, no one has been harmed. Why cause unnecessary pain?

The consequences of his decision are more terrible than his infidelity. Why? Because he has convinced himself that he can live without forgiveness. He has shut himself out of a new beginning. He has decided to live a lie. But his blasphemy "against the Holy Spirit will not be forgiven, either in this age or in the age to come" (12:32).

Jesus' Ministry: Radical Change

Jesus' ministry and the ministry continued by the Holy Spirit in the church assumes that the good news of the Kingdom will make us desire God's will for our lives with all our being. The possibility of a radical change arises from the transforming power released within us by what we treasure in our hearts. Good words, good works, good thoughts come from the good treasure of good hearts. Jesus gave himself to the vocation of revealing the mercy of God so that we might fix our desires upon the kingdom of God and its righteousness. His words and his deeds express his confidence that when we see the goodness of God, we will treasure it in our hearts and be made perfect as God in heaven is perfect.

The life and teaching of Jesus offers the mercy of God to us as God's incredible gift. God wants us to desire God's gifts with such single-minded devotion that our hearts will overflow with the abundance of good treasure. This is truly deliverance from evil. But our experience is not complete until we are consumed by desire for good. Jesus' vocation of saving us from our sins is not accomplished in us until the emptiness of our lives is filled to overflowing by the desire to do God's will.

> Good words, good works, good thoughts come from the good treasure of good hearts.

I was talking one day with a man who is waging a successful struggle against drug addiction. He told me that all his efforts to free himself from this bondage were fruitless until a loving community enabled him to give himself to the goodness in himself and others. To "just say no" was not enough. He also had to discover those things in his life that made him want to say yes!

As I reflect on our conversation now in light of Matthew 12:22-37, I think that he was telling me about a radical change in his life that resulted from the good treasure of his heart. Instead of losing his life in a desperate struggle against evil, he found his life in a wholehearted commitment to good. He was saved from his sins because he could now say yes to his treasure.

Dimension 4:
A Daily Bible Journey Plan

Day 1: Matthew 15:1-20
Day 2: Matthew 15:21-31
Day 3: Matthew 15:32-39
Day 4: Matthew 16:1-20
Day 5: Matthew 16:21-28
Day 6: Matthew 17:1-21
Day 7: Matthew 17:22-27

Matthew 16:13-28

8

THE MINISTRY OF JESUS THE MESSIAH MISUNDERSTOOD: THE NECESSITY OF THE CROSS

Read

This session focuses on Peter's confession that Jesus is the Messiah and on Peter's failure to understand fully what this confession meant. Read Matthew 16:13-28.

Place this passage within its larger context by reading or skimming these passages as well: Jesus' teaching about the ministry of his disciples (9:35–13:53); how Jesus was received by various groups (13:54–14:36); warning about the teaching of the Pharisees (15:11–16:12); necessity of the cross for Jesus and his disciples (16:13–17:23).

What to Watch For
- What people said about Jesus' identity contrasted with what the disciples, represented by Peter, said (16:13-16).
- Peter's confession was based on revelation from the Father in heaven (16:16).
- That which God revealed to Peter and the disciples was the rock upon which Jesus would build his church (16:18).
- The gates of hell would not prevail against the church (16:18).
- Peter and the disciples were given the keys of the kingdom of heaven (16:19).
- Jesus "ordered the disciples not to tell anyone that he was the Messiah" (16:20).
- Jesus showed his disciples "that he must go to Jerusalem and undergo great suffering" at the hands of the Jewish authorities, "and be killed, and on the third day be raised" (16:21).

59

- Jesus rebuked Peter and called him "Satan" when Peter tempted Jesus to deny his vocation (16:23).
- Jesus told his disciples that their vocation required them to deny themselves (16:24).

In this session you will experience the difference between *saying* that "Jesus is the Messiah, the Son of the Living God" and *fully understanding* what Jesus shows us about God's will for his life and the lives of his disciples.

Dimension 1: What Does the Bible Say?

1. What was the difference between what people said about Jesus and what his disciples said? *People — John Baptist, Jeremiah, prophet. Disciples — Son of God*

2. After Peter's confession what did Jesus tell Peter about the church? *Would build it on a rock, gates of Hades could not overcome it*

3. Why did Jesus order the disciples not to tell anyone that he was the Messiah? *Wanted them to wait until the revelation was completed by his resurrection. They did not understand his relationship with God*

4. Why did Peter rebuke Jesus for showing the disciples the necessity of his passion? *He did not understand the plan God had for Jesus*

Dimension 2: What Does the Bible Mean?

Matthew used Peter's confession that Jesus was "the Messiah, the Son of the living God" to remind the church at Antioch about its origin, its vocation, and its accountability. Although Peter had a special place of leadership among the twelve disciples, this Scripture clearly refers to all the disciples and is not limited either to Peter the individual or to the Twelve collectively. The focus of the text is on Jesus and explores his relationship to God, his ministry, and his authority. Matthew feared that the church at Antioch could not understand its life properly unless it kept its attention directed to Jesus, its creator, its teacher, and its judge.

Jesus the Messiah: Creator of the Church

The followers of Jesus were distinguished from people in general by their intimate relationship to him. On occasion, Jesus addressed them directly, rather than impersonally as with the crowds that sometimes listened to Jesus. Therefore, the disciples had a knowledge of Jesus based upon their full participation as his brothers and sisters (Matthew 12:46-50).

People outside the circle of the disciples knew him from a distance. They confused him as being John the Baptist, or Elijah, or Jeremiah, or one of the prophets. Those who had left everything to follow him, who had eaten with him, who had conversed with him, who had received his teaching, and who had been given authority to share his work knew him in an entirely different way.

His followers knew Jesus as he really was. They experienced in him his unique relationship to God. Jesus was with them unconditionally, not because he belonged to them but because he was God's beloved Son. Therefore when Jesus asked them what they thought about his identity, they drew upon their personal experience for his true identity: "You are the Messiah, the Son of the living God" (16:16). Their in-depth acquaintance with him enabled them to make a penetrating judgment about him.

Jesus affirmed what the disciples said about him as the ultimate blessing. It expressed their allegiance to God's goodness as revealed in his words and deeds. Their faith came only because God had opened their eyes and given them speech, not because of any quality or achievement they possessed. They had been transformed by the blessing. The symbol of that transformation was the new name, Peter, which would remind them that their new life together as Jesus' church was built upon the "rock" of the good news of the Kingdom.

Just as Jesus had a special relationship to God, so the church would have a special relationship to heaven. That relationship was possible because the church was always Jesus' possession and creation. Its ability to conquer evil ("the gates of Hades will not prevail against it") resulted from the superior power of the gospel. The authority of the church to preach and teach ("the keys of the kingdom of heaven") depended upon its remaining faithfulness to the revelation of the good news of the Kingdom in the words and deeds of Jesus. No matter how the church responded in faith to the revelation of the Kingdom, it was always subordinate to Jesus and depended upon his teaching for its authority. Therefore, Jesus "sternly ordered them not to tell anyone that he was the Messiah" until the revelation was completed by the Resurrection.

Jesus the Messiah: Teacher of the Church

Jesus "sternly ordered his disciples not to tell anyone that he was the Messiah" (20) because they did not understand that his intimate relationship to God made him value doing God's will more than gaining the approval of the Jewish religious authorities. Jesus' vocation placed him under the obligation of seeking first "the kingdom of God and his righteousness" (6:33). He "began to show his disciples that he must go to Jerusalem and undergo great suffering at the hands of the elders and chief priests and scribes, and be killed, and on the third day be raised" (16:21).

> The Passion is foretold again in Matthew 17:22-23 and 20:17-19.

Matthew wanted to emphasize the critical importance of Jesus' *showing* his disciples the necessity of his Passion. The disciples were not stupid. They simply did not get the point of what Jesus was saying. Rather they had been conditioned to believe that one's special relationship to God resulted in special privilege instead of special responsibility. When Peter rebuked Jesus, saying, "God forbid it, Lord! This must never happen to you" (16:22), he was merely telling Jesus that he could depend on his special relationship to God to save him from all harm. This confrontation between Jesus and Peter picked up the theme of the second temptation (4:5-7). But this new temptation was much more poignant because the voice of Satan was now the voice of Peter, leader of the Twelve and representative of the whole church. Peter expressed a fundamental misunderstanding of the church about Jesus and about its own life. To believe that an intimate relationship to God means special privilege instead of special responsibility is not just a mistaken judgment. It is demonic possession (16:23).

Matthew 16:21 states that "from that time on, Jesus began to *show* his disciples." The disciples could not learn this lesson by words alone. So Jesus *showed* them the truth about God, about himself, and about themselves by a life of self-giving love that authenticated his words. He expected them to *show* that they had learned their lesson thoroughly by joining him in a relationship to God that was expressed in self-giving love. His Passion was the blessing of doing God's will. They could share in the blessing of doing God's will only as his Passion became their passion. What he *showed* his disciples was true for all followers, not just the Twelve. Everything depended upon what they *wanted*. If they *wanted* to avoid conflict with the Jewish authorities, if they *wanted* the rewards of "human things," then they should follow the example of Peter. But if they *wanted* to become Jesus' followers, if they *wanted* the reward of "divine things," then they should follow the example of Jesus.

> The disciples could not learn by words alone. So Jesus *showed* them the truth about God, about himself, and about themselves by a life of self-giving love.

This was the moment of truth for those who *wanted* to be followers of Jesus. The decision Jesus put before them in his words and deeds was whether they would choose to satisfy themselves, claim their privilege, and follow Peter (Satan); or whether they would choose to deny themselves, claim their responsibility, and follow Jesus (God). Peter's way led to death: Jesus' way led to life.

But that was not the way it seemed. From the point of view of "human things," common sense taught that you saved your life by seeking to save it. From the point of view of "divine things," revelation taught that you saved your life by losing it for Jesus' sake, for Jesus' work. Life then was not defined by "human things" but by "divine things." Those who *wanted* "human things" (the whole world) were already dead no matter what they seemed to have. Those who *wanted* "divine things" (the kingdom of God) had found their life no matter what they seemed to lack.

Jesus the Messiah: Judge of the Church

Matthew used these traditions to help the church at Antioch *want* "divine things" more than "human things." If the church preoccupied itself with its human origins and its social relationships, then it would forget that Jesus was the one who built the church and who gave the church its authority to minister. Matthew wanted to keep the church true to its founder and faithful to its mission by centering the attention of the church upon "divine things."

In his most powerful appeal, Matthew reminded the church that those who had power to kill the body had no power to kill the soul (10:26-33). The fact that after Jesus had suffered "at the hands of the elders and chief priests and scribes," and was killed, and "on the third day" was raised provided the clearest evidence. Christians in Antioch could live without fear of the human powers that killed Jesus' body but not his soul, his real life with God.

Whom, then, should they fear? They should fear God. God would judge everyone, sending the risen Jesus as the final judge of the last days to "repay everyone for what had been done."

The confession of the disciples in words had to be confirmed in deeds. Peter had to do more than simply say about Jesus, "You are the Messiah, the Son of the living God." Peter also had to *want* what Jesus *wanted*, "divine things" rather than "human things." If Peter *wanted divine things*, he would be rewarded with life. If he *wanted human things*, he would be rewarded with death. The Final Judgment was not an arbitrary action of God, but simply the bringing to light of the allegiance of the heart. What people *really wanted* was what people would *really receive*, either "human things" or "divine things."

Matthew used these traditions about Peter's confession and Jesus' teaching about the way of discipleship to help the church at Antioch *want* to be followers of Jesus. His strategy included warning about the ultimate consequences of choices. But finally he based his appeal not upon warning but upon affirmation of the victory of "divine things" over "human things" in the resurrection of Jesus. No matter how frail the performance of the church, no matter how halting the confession of the church, what God had done in Jesus the Messiah could not be undone. It was possible for the church to *want* to be his disciples because in every generation there were "some standing here who will not taste death before they see the Son of Man coming in his kingdom" (16:28).

Dimension 3: What Does the Bible Mean to Us?

The church today is often tempted to follow the example of Peter by setting its "mind not on divine things but on human things." This temptation expresses itself in our tendency to define our lives and to understand our vocation in light of our human origins and our social relationships. To the extent that the church seeks to avoid any conflict with the dominant forces in our society and to maintain our status as a respected institution within society, we are in danger of forgetting what gives us our distinctive identity and mission. We are not likely to be aware of this threat to our integrity or to be able to resist it unless we pay close attention to Matthew's witness to Jesus as the creator, teacher, and judge of the church.

Jesus the Messiah: Creator of the Church

Today's church still faces the question of who Jesus is. We can never just repeat what others have said about Jesus. We are asked directly and personally, "But who do *you* say that I am?" We cannot even simply repeat Peter's affirmation. The ultimate allegiance of our hearts is at stake.

> We can never just repeat what others have said about Jesus. We are asked directly and personally, "But who do *you* say that I am?" We cannot even simply repeat Peter's affirmation. The ultimate allegiance of our hearts is at stake.

No one can make our affirmation for us. We have been blessed by the revelation of God's goodness in Jesus so that we can acknowledge his claim upon our lives by choosing the kingdom of God as the treasure of our hearts. Whatever our words, whatever the details of our encounter with the revelation, we know who he is when our hearts are given over to God who is revealed in him.

Jesus built the church upon the "rock" of the good news of the Kingdom that we experience in a variety of ways. That which gives us hope in the presence of evil is not the form of our expression about who Jesus is nor the details of our experience of him. Rather it is the truth we discovered in the first chapter of Matthew's Gospel: the reality of Emmanuel, God with us.

We witness God's presence in Jesus by affirming the goodness of this revelation of God in Jesus. This revelation may well inspire other persons to make their own affirmation in their own words and in the light of their experience. We dare not force others to repeat our words or to conform to our experience of God.

My wife and I were worshiping in our church with a young Muslim. When we came to the celebration of Holy Communion, my wife explained the Christian ritual and indicated that we would understand his not wanting to participate. He surprised us by saying that he wanted to commune with us, and we quickly assured him that he was welcome at the Lord's Table. This experience has left us with many unanswered questions and has made us take a hard look at many of the exclusive ideas and practices that have been promoted in the name of Jesus.

Jesus the Messiah: Teacher of the Church

We still want to respond with Peter by saying, "God forbid it, Lord! This must never happen to you." But Jesus showed us in his words and deeds that when we choose God as the treasure of our hearts, our intimate relationship to God does not give us *privilege* but *responsibility*.

Our relationship to God through Jesus does not make us superior to other people. Our relationship does not entitle us to coerce and control people. Our relationship does not authorize us to condemn and exclude others. Instead, our relationship transforms us so that we want nothing more than our relationship with God, and we will to do what God requires. Jesus shows us that the way to life is the way of self-giving love, and he shows us how to find life by losing it.

We cannot make what Jesus shows us conform to what the world teaches us. Too often the church has chosen like Peter to set its "mind not on divine things but on human things." This is the tragedy of the history of the church. When that happens, the church ceases to be the church and loses its life by seeking to save it.

I remember a conversation that I had years ago with a wealthy and influential member of a church in a rapidly changing inner-city neighborhood. As we talked, he told me of the past "greatness" of *his* church and how he was committed to keeping *his* church as it had always been: white, upper-middle class, affluent, and influential. We talked about the challenge of a racially mixed neighborhood and the opportunity for the church to model an integrated community. His parting comment to me was, "It's *my* church, and *I* will decide who is welcome."

This tragedy repeats itself when we presume to think that we really know who Jesus is by telling people about him instead of learning who he is by becoming like him in ministry.

Jesus the Messiah: Judge of the Church

When the risen Lord comes at the end of the age to judge the church, his disciples will be repaid not for what they have said about him but "for what has been done." Matthew 16:27 states this warning clearly. Those who have set their mind on "human things" will get the reward of their choice: death. Those who have set their mind on "divine things" will get the reward of their choice: life.

God *wants* us to *want* good instead of evil. All that Jesus is and all that he says and does is intended to make us *want* the good more than we want the whole world. The good is not some abstract idea. It is the self-giving love of God that Jesus showed in his suffering, death, and resurrection.

We hope, then, for the church and for the world to rest ultimately upon the presence of the risen Lord with us. That presence cannot be defeated, cannot be removed, cannot be denied because it is God's last word. The last word is *life*, not death. The victorious Lord is none other than the crucified Jesus. We enter into his victory not only by confessing with our lips but by following with our deeds. The glory of church history is revealed in faithful disciples who have denied themselves, taken up their cross, and followed him.

Celebrate with me the group of Christian women in our town who have taken upon themselves a ministry to the people in our nursing homes. One woman in particular is a registered nurse in a convalescent home. She takes her day off from work to be a part of this ministry. No one could pay any of these women to do what they do. It is true that they are blessed with good feelings by what they do. But they do it not because of anything they get. They do it because they *want* to do it. And they *want* to do it because "they see the Son of Man coming in his kingdom."

Dimension 4:
A Daily Bible Journey Plan

Day 1: Matthew 18:1-14
Day 2: Matthew 18:15-22
Day 3: Matthew 18:23-35
Day 4: Matthew 19:1-12
Day 5: Matthew 19:13-30
Day 6: Matthew 20:1-16
Day 7: Matthew 20:17-28

9

Matthew 19:13-30

THE MINISTRY OF JESUS THE MESSIAH DENIED: THE GRIEF OF SELF-RELIANCE

This session focuses on Matthew 19:13-30. These verses sit within the broader context of Matthew 17:24–20:16, which shows Jesus on his way to Jerusalem, stopping briefly at Capernaum and continuing his journey through the region of Judea beyond the Jordan.

> Read Matthew 19:13-30 to deepen your awareness of the importance of staying in community and the results of choosing to live in isolation.

In the first section (17:24–18:35) Jesus taught his disciples about the importance of maintaining relationships in the community by humbly submitting to the needs of others. In the second section (19:1–20:16), he elaborated on this theme by showing that only those who *want* to maintain relationships with others will be empowered to do so.

What to Watch For

- When people brought little children to Jesus for blessing, Jesus' disciples attempted to turn the children away. Jesus, however, declared that the kingdom of heaven belongs to little children and blessed them (19:13-15).
- When someone pressed Jesus on what kind of good deed would earn eternal life, Jesus specified commandments that deal with human relationships. When the man pressed Jesus further, he responded that if he wished to be perfect, he should sell his possessions, give the money to the poor, and have treasure in heaven. Then he invited him to come and follow him. The young man heard Jesus but went away grieving because he had many possessions. Someone asked Jesus what good deed must be done to have eternal life (19:16-21).

- Jesus told his disciples that it was impossible for the rich to enter the kingdom of God. When the disciples asked who could be saved, Jesus answered that it was impossible for mortals but not for God (19:23-26).
- When Peter asked Jesus what the disciples would receive for leaving everything to follow him, Jesus told them they would share his throne and his judgment in the last days, be included in the true family of God, and inherit eternal life; however, many who were first would be last, and the last would be first (19:27-30).

In this session you will see how "the little children" offer us the community we need, without which our lives are grief-stricken.

Dimension 1: What Does the Bible Say?

1. Who are "the little children" who were being brought for his blessing?

2. Why did the disciples speak sternly to those who brought "the little children"?

3. Why did the young man's many possessions cause him to grieve when he heard Jesus' word?

4. What was Peter told that the disciples would have because they had left everything to follow Jesus?

Dimension 2: What Does the Bible Mean?

Who were "the little children" (Matthew 19:13)? They were not only infants. They included all those of any age who came to Jesus or were brought to Jesus because they were sick, possessed by demons, excluded from society, or bowed down with any kind of heavy burden.

The words *children* and *little ones* were used as synonyms throughout the section of Matthew's Gospel where Jesus taught about the importance of community. Children were to be given the highest priority in the community. They embodied the humility required of all persons who entered the kingdom of heaven. The humility represented in a child provided the measure of greatness in the Kingdom. To welcome "one such child" was to welcome Jesus himself (18:1-5).

Nothing disciples could do to maintain the community of faith was more important than including the "little ones." The worst thing a disciple could do was to cause a "little one" to stumble (18:6-7). To cause a "little one" to stumble was a sin to be avoided at all cost (18:8-9). Christians consider the "little ones" as infinitely precious because God cherishes them and wants them included in the community (18:10-14).

God intended the community of faith to need all its members. Christians, therefore, were under obligation to restore any member (little one) who sinned. The obligation to include others was so great that no limit could be placed on the requirement to forgive (18:15-22). The most damning failure of Matthew's Christian community was when it failed to forgive someone. Those moments revealed that the community treasured its own privilege and its own "rightness" more than it treasured the "little ones" (18:23-35).

The "little ones"—the little children—appear in Matthew 19:13 as those who confront the disciples with what they need, what they must become, and what they will receive as their reward in the Last Judgment. The behavior of the disciples toward the children shock many readers of Matthew's Gospel. Although Jesus carefully instructed the disciples about the decisive importance of receiving the children, they still didn't seem to get it. What was their problem? Were they slow learners? Or was the problem more serious?

The Little Children: What Disciples Need

The conversation between Jesus and his disciples begun in Matthew 19:10 is abruptly interrupted in verse 13. Anonymous people cause the interruption by bringing little children to Jesus "that he might lay his hands on them and pray." We may reasonably speculate that these unknown people had heard about Jesus and had concluded that Jesus would welcome and bless the little children. Because of what we have already read about Jesus' teachings and deeds, we expect Jesus would respond to the needs of the little children. The behavior of the disciples, however, breaks the expected sequence of events. The disciples acted as if Jesus had more important concerns than the little children. They assumed that Jesus did not want to be bothered by these children. In spite of what they had been taught from the beginning of their life with Jesus and had been shown in his words and deeds about his ministry, the disciples still did not know who Jesus was and what he wanted to do.

A rebuke appears in this passage, just as in session 8. The New Revised Standard Version's usage of the phrase *spoke sternly* in Matthew 19:13 conceals the fact that the disciples rebuked those who brought the little children to Jesus in the same way that Peter rebuked Jesus when he began to show them the necessity of his cross. The same issue has been raised again. And in this passage as in Matthew 16:21-23, the disciples revealed in their words and their actions that their mind was not set "on divine things but on human things." They valued their own privilege and status more than they valued the little children.

> The disciples turned the little children away because they did not recognize that their deepest need was to be with the little children.

The disciples thought they needed to be with someone who was powerful and authoritative, someone who could give them power and authority. Perhaps Jesus was that someone! Therefore they sought to protect themselves from the little children who had neither power nor authority. The disciples feared that the helplessness of these little children would interfere with their own sense of status and privilege. They "despised" the "little ones," not seeing that they could not be with God without being with the "little ones" (18:10-14).

The contrast between what the disciples said and did and what Jesus said and did helps us see more clearly the meaning of this passage. "But Jesus said, 'Let the little children come to me, and do not stop them; for it is to such as these that the kingdom of heaven belongs,' And he laid his hands on them and went on his way" (19:14-15). Jesus' action confirmed his words. He did not speak to them and go on his way. He identified with them. "He lay his hands on them." He touched them and blessed them. Other passages tell how he took their infirmities and bore their diseases because he was gentle and humble in heart (8:17; 11:29). Because he wanted God's promised salvation to be fulfilled in his words and deeds, he was their Emmanuel, "God is with us."

The Little Children: What Disciples Must Become

Again something interrupts the narrative. This time someone came and asked Jesus what seemed to be an unrelated question, "Teacher, what good deed must I do to have eternal life?" Jesus told him what he already knew: that God was good, and that one entered life by keeping God's commandments. "Which ones?" the man asked. In reply Jesus lifted up the commandments dealing with human relationships. He emphasized loving one's neighbor as one's self. The young man claimed to have kept them all and asked, "What do I still lack?" Jesus told him, "If you wish to be perfect, go, sell your possessions, and give the money to the poor, and you will have treasure in heaven; then come, follow me." When the young man heard Jesus' word, "he went away grieving, for he had many possessions" (16:22).

The young man contrasts strikingly with the children earlier in this chapter. The children were brought; the young man came on his own initiative. The children waited silently in the background; the young man moved assertively into the foreground of the action. The children depended upon others; the young man was independent. The children were powerless; the young man was powerful (Luke 18 even describes him as a ruler).

The dialogue revealed the young man to be a person in control, determined to remain in control. He went away grieving when Jesus told him he lacked a center of control beyond himself. Jesus confronted him with the fact that he needed "the poor." He could not live "eternally" without "the little ones." Jesus recognized that the man's problem was that he valued his many possessions more than he valued those "little ones." His heart was set on earthly treasure rather than on heavenly treasure. He did not *want* to be perfect; he did not *want* to be generous as God was generous. Therefore he could not do what he did not *want* to do. Presumably he kept his possessions, gave no money to the poor, had treasure on earth, and followed his own way.

The young man sought to save himself and lost himself. When he shut the poor (the children) out of his life, he lost his life. Everything he did was destined to fail because he *wanted* the wrong thing. He *wanted* to be superior to the children and therefore rejected what they offered him. He *wanted* to be different from them and therefore resisted the invitation to become one of them. But at least he caught a glimpse of another possibility. That glimpse was not enough to make him *want* to follow Jesus into the Kingdom as a little child, but it was enough to make him grieve as he went on his way relying upon himself.

The young man was a mirror in which would-be disciples could behold their basic problem. They, too, *wanted* the wrong thing. Wanting the wrong thing was the reason the young man went away grieving. Wanting the wrong thing was the reason it was as impossible for a rich man to enter the kingdom of God as for a camel to go through the eye of a needle. The basic truth came crashing in upon the disciples and left them at the brink of despair. If salvation was dependent upon what people *wanted* and if people *wanted* the wrong thing, then who could be saved?

> Anybody can be saved because God is at work in Jesus helping people to want the right thing.

The answer was that anybody could be saved because God was at work in Jesus helping people to *want* the right thing. The good news of the Kingdom could even make rich people desire treasure in heaven more than treasure on earth. God created these impossible possibilities. God could even make Peter into a little child.

The Little Children: What Disciples Will Receive

In verse 27, Peter spoke for ideal disciples who had done what the young man had failed to do. Their reward was that they received what they really *wanted*.

They would be with Jesus not just on earth but in heaven. They participated in his royal power by giving up all worldly power. They were with Jesus throughout eternity because on earth they had welcomed the little children, become little children, and joined the family of those who did the will of God.

To many readers, Matthew 19:28-30 sounds frightening with its words about eternal life and the Last Judgment. It was not intended to frighten or warn "wannabe" disciples, but to attract them and make them *want* to include the "little children" as essential members of the community. Those who lost their lives in humble service would indeed find their lives in a community no longer built upon status and privilege but upon humility and responsibility.

The defining presence of the little children symbolized the radical difference between the community of disciples and the community of the world. Throughout this entire section Jesus consistently showed his disciples in word and deed that they needed to welcome the children in order to be with him and to participate in his ministry. He also helped them understand that they could not *do* what they ought to do unless they *became* what they ought to be. God's giving of God's self in Jesus was the only power that could make them become like little children by leaving everything to follow Jesus. Jesus' ironic statement summarized this radical reversal of life in the community: "But many who are first will be last, and the last will be first" (30). This teaching did not mean what it seemed to say. It did not mean a revolution in the community of disciples that would simply reverse roles so that those who were first would be last and those who were last would be first. It meant rather that, in the new community, all the distinctions of the world were made obsolete by the fact that all were children of God and brothers and sisters of Jesus. Since all persons were blessed by being members of the community, the distinctions *first* and *last* no longer had meaning.

Dimension 3:
What Does the Bible Mean to Us?

This hard teaching of Jesus is not optional. We need first to give up that notion in order to apply the biblical truth to our own situation. If we really *want* to be disciples, if we really *want* to receive the kingdom of God, if we really *want* to have eternal life, then we *must* hear and do what Jesus taught about receiving the little children. If we do not include the children, then our action reveals that we *want* to go our own way more than we *want* to follow Jesus, that we *want* to exercise our own power more than the power of the Kingdom, and that we *want* our own possessions more than eternal life.

The Little Children: What Disciples Need

We need the little children more than they need us. We cannot be the agents of God's salvation in the world without giving the children the highest priority in our lives. When children are brought to us, we need to recognize that they are God's gift to us. But this gift has strings attached!

We cannot receive the little children without leaving everything else. Only then will our actions reveal that we value the children more highly than we value all our possessions. We cannot receive the children and at the same time keep our possessions, control our lives, and protect ourselves. If we *want* to receive the children, we must deny ourselves and take up our cross and follow Jesus.

Our community is currently engaged in a heated debate about a bond issue to provide adequate educational facilities for our children. The children have been brought to us as God's good gift. Our vote on the bond issue will reveal what we really *want* in our community. A vote against the bond issue can always be rationalized and justified as good stewardship and responsible allocation of limited funds. A vote for the bond issue can be promoted as an optional matter, something we ought to do to meet the needs of the children.

The text from Matthew's Gospel seems to say that no matter how we vote on the bond issue, we have an opportunity to recognize that we need the children more than they need us. Our votes should reflect the fact that we *want* to include the children more than we want to protect our power and our property.

The Little Children: What Disciples Must Become

A false image will hinder us as we seek to be followers of Jesus. Our society encourages us to view ourselves as aggressive, competitive, and independent. Jesus seeks to create a community in which we give up aggression for humility, competition for cooperation, and independence for dependence. Becoming like a little child involves this kind of attitudinal transformation, at least in part. Jesus invites us to forsake the false self-image of this society and to see ourselves as we really are, God's little ones: "Come to me, all you that are weary and are carrying heavy burdens, and I will give you rest" (11:28).

A few years ago a friend of mine tried to help his family through a crisis. He saw himself as the rock upon whom others could depend. He thought of himself as the person in control. He gave rather than received.

At a particularly trying moment he and his wife were talking to their son. He put on his usual mask of self-sufficiency. Suddenly, his son reached out and embraced him and his wife and said, "I love you both more than I can ever say." Then he turned to his mother and said, "Mom, take care of Dad."

My friend told me later that he suddenly felt awash in great relief. He was free to be himself. He realized he could receive help. He could become a "little child." He no longer needed to bear the heavy burden of his false self-image.

The Little Children: What Disciples Will Receive

God's gift to the world is the gift of self-giving love in Jesus. Disciples receive that love, serve it, and find themselves transformed by it. This love is not an abstract idea; rather it is concretely experienced in a community composed of Jesus' brothers and sisters. Disciples enjoy their rewards on earth and in heaven in the relationships of the family of God.

Disciples treasure their relationships with the children more than anything else. A few months ago a friend had a heated exchange with a person whom she had known and loved for a long time. As a result of the confrontation, the other person felt alienated and mistreated. My friend had spoken in defense of her principles and her own integrity. She felt certain that she had not done anything wrong; the other person had responded inappropriately. She told me that as long as she considered the event from the perspective of her own status and privilege, there was nothing she could do about the situation. Then she began to think about the need she had to be in relation with her estranged friend. She finally came to the conclusion that her relationship to the other person was what she really *wanted* more than self-justification and more than her own principles. She found her reward not in vindication but in reconciliation within the family of God with one of the little children.

Dimension 4:
A Daily Bible Journey Plan

> Day 1: Matthew 20:29-34
> Day 2: Matthew 21:1-11
> Day 3: Matthew 21:12-22
> Day 4: Matthew 21:23-32
> Day 5: Matthew 21:33-46
> Day 6: Matthew 22:1-14
> Day 7: Matthew 22:15-22

10

Matthew 21:1-17

The Ministry of Jesus the Messiah Affirmed: The Praise of Babies

Matthew 21:1-17 develops dramatically the theme of misunderstanding Jesus' ministry. In this passage, Jesus enters Jerusalem. He is welcomed by the crowds, opposed by the chief priests and the scribes in the Temple, and praised by the children. The difference between Jesus' behavior and the behavior that is expected of him creates great tension.

What to Watch For
- Jesus rode into Jerusalem on a donkey and a colt to fulfill the prophecy of Zechariah 9:9 (21:7).
- The crowds greeted Jesus as the Son of David, although they seemed not really to know who Jesus was (21:9-10).
- Jesus drove the merchants and money changers from the Temple because they had made the "house of prayer" into a "den of robbers" (21:12-13).
- Jesus healed the blind and the lame in the Temple (21:14).
- The chief priests and the scribes became angry when they heard the children praise Jesus (21:15).

In this session, you will experience the mercy of Jesus' ministry as the basis for knowing and affirming who he is.

Dimension 1:
What Does the Bible Say?

1. What was the significance of Jesus' riding into Jerusalem on a donkey and a colt? *Fullfill prophecy*

2. How did the crowds understand Jesus' entry into Jerusalem when they greeted him as the Son of David?

3. Why did Jesus drive the money changers and merchants from the Temple? *Was house of prayer Merchants not honest Cheating people*

4. What was the significance of Jesus' healing the blind and the lame who came to him in the Temple?

5. Why did the chief priests and the scribes become angry when the children praised Jesus as the Son of David?

6. Why was the praise of the children acceptable to Jesus?

Dimension 2:
What Does the Bible Mean?

This text emphasizes that Jesus is a royal figure, the Son of David; it also underscores that he is not the Davidic king of popular expectations. One should not hear the greeting of the crowds uncritically. Although they said the right words about Jesus, they did not know him as he really was nor follow him as true disciples. The biblical text challenges the reader to understand what kind of king Jesus was, to see how he exercised his royal authority, and to join the little children ("nursing babies") in his praise.

Jesus: The King of Peace

Jesus approached Jerusalem; but his center of operation was outside the city at the Mount of Olives. According to Zechariah 14, the Messiah would appear at the Mount of Olives in the last days. Jesus was less comfortable with the religious authorities of Jerusalem than with his community of followers on the Mount of Olives. Jesus' future did not depend on his reception in Jerusalem but rather Jerusalem's future depended upon its reception of Jesus.

In this passage (Matthew 21:1-17), fundamental questions about *ownership* arose. Since God created all things, all things belonged to God and were subject to God's will. Jesus sent his disciples to take possession of a donkey and a colt. Jesus chose to ride into Jerusalem on a donkey and a colt as a sign that his Kingdom was from God and was subject to God's will. As the Messiah of God, Jesus rode into Jerusalem as the King of Peace whose purpose was to establish peace by renouncing the instruments of war. He did not ride into Jerusalem as a conquering hero on a war horse but as the meek, gentle Son of the living God on a beast of burden. Jesus entered Jerusalem to claim the city, its people, and its institutions for God.

> **Mount of Olives -** A high ridge about two and a half miles in length, part of the central north-south mountain range that runs through Palestine. Jesus' place of lodging during his last days was probably in Bethany on the Mount of Olives. His teaching concerning the end of the age is associated with the Mount of Olives (Matthew 24:3–25:46).

The crowd that had traveled with Jesus on his way from Galilee to Jerusalem recognized Jesus as their king. They prepared Jesus' way by spreading cloaks and tree branches on the road. They also shouted greetings to him as they went before him and followed him into the city.

This crowd said the right words,

"Hosanna to the Son of David!

Blessed is the one who comes in the name of the Lord!"

They did not know who Jesus really was because they were preoccupied with their own status and privilege. They had just revealed their misunderstanding of Jesus by rebuking the blind men who called out for mercy (20:31). And they soon would join Jesus' persecutors and cry out for his execution (27:15-23). Although Jesus was the longed for Davidic king, he was not the military conqueror the crowd expected. Instead Jesus was God's king, the agent of God's mercy to all who had been excluded and neglected (9:13; 12:7).

The narrative carries forward the themes introduced earlier in Matthew 16:13-28. The disciples and the crowd appeared to follow Jesus. They seemed to know who he was because they knew enough to say the right words about him. But the right words concealed the fact that they had not understood that Jesus' special relationship to God presented him with special responsibility for others. They also failed to comprehend that their special relationship to Jesus required that they, too, accept a special responsibility to serve others. Therefore Jesus showed them that they must confirm their affirmations about him by denying themselves, taking up their cross, and following him. Only those persons who followed Jesus to the cross would know that he was more than a prophet from Galilee (21:10-11).

Jesus: The Servant of God

Jesus' destination as he entered Jerusalem was the Temple. The Temple symbolized the dedication of the people to God and their obedience to God's will as revealed in Scripture. Jesus' action in the Temple did not reject the importance of the Temple nor the revelation of Scripture. He drove the money changers and the merchants from the Temple because they misused their power and privilege to benefit themselves rather than to glorify God. The problem was not with the Temple or with Scripture.

The problem was with people whose hard hearts excluded the needy people from the Temple and who used Scripture to justify that exclusion. Jesus appealed to Scripture to condemn their action and to show them the kind of action God wanted in the Temple.

The Temple symbolized that everything belonged to God and was created for God's purposes. God desired *mercy*, not *sacrifice*. Jesus expressed God's desire for mercy in Matthew 9:13 and 12:7 by quoting from Hosea 6:6. Those who used Scripture to promote sacrifice in the Temple were hard of heart. They did not glorify God but used Scripture to rob God and to protect themselves. God's house belonged instead to the little children, to the little ones, to persons suffering infirmities, to the poor. Whatever was taken from them or denied to them was robbery. Those who claimed to honor God but who excluded the little children were dishonoring God, profaning the Temple, and indulging themselves.

The Temple authorities misused Scripture when they blocked persons who needed mercy from access to God. The basic prayer of the little ones, the little children, the poor was, "Have mercy on us, Lord!" That prayer could not be heard in the Temple in Jerusalem because those who were in charge had used Scripture to declare that "the blind and the lame shall not come into the house" (2 Samuel 5:8). They were so concerned with promoting their own religious rites, collecting the Temple tax, and requiring sacrifice that they had neither the will nor the ability to practice mercy.

Jesus countered their misuse of Scripture by quoting a passage that claimed the Temple for God and God's little ones while denouncing the religious authorities as robbers (Isaiah 56:7; Jeremiah 7:11). Jesus interpreted Scripture as including others. He did not act impulsively in the Temple, but with the same kind of submission to the will of God in Scripture that had sustained him in his encounter with Satan (Matthew 4:1-11).

Jesus: The King of Babies

This passage comes to a climax with the praise voiced by the children in the Temple. They knew who Jesus really was because they experienced his compassion. Jesus entered the Temple as the one who took upon himself the infirmities and diseases of the little ones. He was the king who said to them in his words and deeds, "Come to me, all you that are weary and are carrying heavy burdens, and I will give you rest. Take my yoke upon you, and learn from me; for I am gentle and humble in heart, and you will find rest for your souls. For my yoke is easy, and my burden is light" (11:28-30). This king asked nothing from them, exacted no tax from them, did not lord it over them, but gave himself for them.

> Jesus justified his action by saying to his opponents, "It is written, 'My house shall be called a house of prayer'; but you are making it a den of robbers."

Jesus showed the Temple authorities the right thing to do in the Temple: he cured persons of their blindness and lameness. The response of the children was the right response. They praised him in the Temple because they had received mercy from him. They acknowledged him as king, not because he was a conquering hero or an oppressive ruler but because he was a servant who gave his life for them. They said the right words with the right understanding, "Hosanna to the Son of David!" He was the authentic king and they were his authentic subjects. Those who recognized their need and came to him to be cured were transformed by his compassion into the little ones who praised him and followed him.

When the chief priests and the scribes heard the children praise Jesus, they became angry. Jesus denounced them for failing to show mercy to those who were in need. Because Jesus was merciful, the children acclaimed him as king. Jesus confronted all who were in the Temple with a clear voice. Either they renounce everything to follow Jesus into the kingdom of heaven or cling to their own status and power and turn away from Jesus in anger.

The children represented ideal disciples. They symbolized those who came to Jesus in their need and who had been transformed by his mercy. Their acclamation of Jesus came from the heart. They had been cured of all obstacles that had prevented their following Jesus. They *wanted* to follow him more than they *wanted* anything else. They left everything to follow him. They did so not because they had been coerced and manipulated by an oppressive ruler, but because they had been transformed by the incredible power of his compassion.

Jesus recognized the praise of the children in the Temple as the response of persons who had been cured. He told the angry chief priests and scribes that if they had not been blinded by their misuse of Scripture and crippled by their hardness of heart, they would have heard the praise of the children as worship hallowing God's name in God's house. Just as Jesus ful-

> "Out of the mouths of babes and infants you have founded a bulwark because of your foes" (Psalm 8:2).

filled Scripture by driving the merchants and money changers from the Temple and by healing the blind and the lame, so the children fulfilled Scripture by crying, "Hosanna to the Son of David."

Dimension 3: What Does the Bible Mean to Us?

This lesson helps us recognize Jesus as our King as we experience anew his compassion for us. When we come to Jesus with our needs, he welcomes us and cures us. When we do not recognize our own needs and we refuse to be cured by him, we are guilty of hardness of heart. Since we do not understand that we are in need of mercy, we resent those who do receive mercy. The praise of the little children angers us because it confronts us with a different perception of God. The questions this text raises for us are, Do we really know who Jesus is? Is our praise acceptable to him?

Jesus: The King of Peace

We know that this lesson is beginning to have the right effect on us when we start to experience the difference between how Jesus comes into our lives and the way we expect him to come.

In this passage Jesus challenges all our claims of ownership. We own nothing absolutely. God claims everything we are and have. Any expression of our allegiance to Jesus not accompanied by a conscious decision to give up everything is a denial of Jesus' claim upon our lives. If we use Jesus to claim special privilege for ourselves and to protect our own possessions, then we have joined the crowd that cried, "Hosanna to the Son of David!" but refused to follow him to the cross.

Jesus always comes into our lives as the King of Peace who is gentle and humble in heart. To the extent that we persist in injustices that explode into violence, we are not his followers. The problem is that we greet him with the right words but reject him with the wrong actions. For example, we value our own national self-interest more than we value the kingdom of heaven. We trust our own military might more than we trust the goodness of God. We want the security of isolation more than the peace of community.

A few years ago one of the women's organizations in our church was planning its program for the coming year. One woman proposed a program on world peace. A long discussion followed in which some persons argued that world peace was too political a topic for their group to consider. Some strongly opposed the subject as controversial and divisive. World peace was about to be rejected as a program for the group.

A young mother spoke up. She saw nothing controversial about being for peace. She asked who would like to see her two sons killed in a war.

Then she said quietly that she did not see how the group could claim to be Christian and not support the cause of world peace.

Jesus: The Servant of God

This text speaks to those of us who give our resources to maintain churches. Jesus' words and deeds show that all religious institutions belong to God and must be judged by how they conform to God's purposes. If we lose sight of this fundamental truth, then we are likely to claim our churches for our own purposes.

We cannot simply acknowledge that our churches belong to God. Most of us would quickly agree with the statement that our church is God's house. But can you also agree that when God claims your church as God's house, God identifies and includes in it those persons on the margins of our society?

This passage presents a clear, challenging picture of the kind of activity pleasing to God in God's house. The money changers were driven from the Temple not because they were ritually incorrect but because they were morally bankrupt. Nor should we consider our rituals as ends in themselves. They must be evaluated on how they help us to acknowledge God's ownership of our lives and how they equip us to serve as agents of God's mercy. The standard we should invoke as we evaluate our worship is not whether it makes us feel good but whether it makes us want to welcome the least people in our society as our brothers and sisters in Christ.

> When we exclude any group of God's little ones from our compassion, then we transform God's house of prayer into a den of robbers.

This text leaves no room for neutrality. Either the churches where we worship and serve are God's house where the prayers of God's little ones are heard and answered, or they are dens of robbers where the powerful voices of special privilege drown out the cries of the little ones. No amount of tinkering with the organization or rewriting the rules will reform a church that has become a den of robbers. What is required is a new experience of God's mercy as God makes us aware that *we* are the little ones and gives us the will to identify with the little ones as members of God's household.

Jesus: The King of Babies

This session confronts those who are angry because their special privilege has been challenged by the mercy of Jesus. It invites them to become little children who rejoice because they have received his mercy. Since most of us are closer to the chief priests and the scribes than we are to the children, we cannot become like the children without going through a radical transformation.

We must leave certain things in order to become like the children. We must leave our prejudices against those who are different. We must leave the idea of excluding others. We must leave our preoccupation with the privileges that we claim because of our status and power. We must leave the notion that God cares for us more than God cares for all the little ones.

> This text leaves no room for neutrality. Either the churches where we worship and serve are God's house where the prayers of God's little ones are heard and answered, or they are dens of robbers where the powerful voices of special privilege drown out the cries of the little ones.

To be transformed by an experience of the mercy of Jesus is to want to follow him. Following him means that we join him in trusting the goodness of God. Following him means caring for each other. Following him means valuing our relationship to God more than we value anything else. Following him means becoming a blessing for others.

I have been thinking about the praise of babies all through the writing of this chapter. The children in our children's choir keep coming to the center of my thoughts. They summarize the meaning of this text for me.

The participation of our children's choir in our worship is no longer relegated to an occasional appearance to entertain the adults and to give the parents a special reason for coming to church. Their singing has become a model for all would-be disciples. In them I behold the ideal disciple who has been transformed into a little child and who has left everything to follow Jesus. They remind me that Jesus is always present with us as a little child. Only those who become little children know who Jesus really is and how to praise him.

Dimension 4:
A Daily Bible Journey Plan

Day 1: Matthew 22:23-33

Day 2: Matthew 22:34-46

Day 3: Matthew 23:1-15

Day 4: Matthew 23:16-26

Day 5: Matthew 23:27-36

Day 6: Matthew 23:37-39

Day 7: Matthew 24:1-8

Matthew 25:31-46

11

THE MINISTRY OF JESUS THE MESSIAH NOW AND NOT YET: THE COMING JUDGMENT

Matthew 25:31-46 develops the themes introduced by Jesus' entrance into Jerusalem. In the immediately preceding passages, the conflict between Jesus and the religious leaders in Jerusalem about his authority unfolded in the Temple (21:23-27). By relying on the power of God, he thwarted their attempts to trap him (21:28–22:46). He warned his disciples and the crowds not to follow the Jerusalem leaders because they were hypocrites more concerned with protecting themselves than with doing the will of God (23:1-39). Then he cautioned his disciples not to be misled by false leaders within the church who thought they could avoid the judgment of his presence by speculating about the time of his coming (24:1–25:30).

Although you may wish to read or skim the preceding passages, be sure to read Matthew 25:31-46, in which Jesus warned about the judgment of the nations when the Son of man will come in glory.

What to Watch For
- At the Final Judgment the Son of man will judge all the nations (25:31-32).
- The blessing of the Kingdom will come upon those who ministered to the Son of man when he was hungry, thirsty, a stranger, naked, sick, and a prisoner, although they will be surprised that they have ministered to the Son of man (25:34-40).
- Those who did not minister to the Son of man at these times will receive the curse of eternal punishment, although they, too, will be surprised that they failed to minister to him (25:41-46).

In this chapter you will prepare for the end by learning how to live now as if the Son of man had already come in glory.

83

Dimension 1: What Does the Bible Say?

1. What is the "glory" of the Son of man?

   God's power

2. To whom does "all the nations" refer?

   all humanity

3. Why were the sheep and the goats equally surprised by the basis of their judgment?

4. Who are "the least of these"?

Dimension 2: What Does the Bible Mean?

Some Christians of the church in Antioch thought that because they had been instructed in the mysteries of the kingdom of God, they would have a special advantage at the Last Judgment. They thought they would be judged on what they had said about Jesus rather than on how they had obeyed his teaching. Matthew 25:31-46 corrects that misunderstanding by presenting the Last Judgment as a universal day of reckoning based upon how people have or have not practiced mercy. Just as Jesus, the humble and lowly Son of man, had ignored all distinctions between insiders and outsiders during his earthly ministry, so Jesus, the majestic and exalted Son of man, would ignore all distinctions between insiders and outsiders when he came in his glory.

In a real sense the Last Judgment had already come. The glorious Judge of the Last Days was already present in the hungry, the thirsty, the stranger, the naked, the sick, and the prisoner. Those who acknowledged him in the *now* of his humility and gentleness would be acknowledged by him in the *not yet* of his glory and power. Those who rejected him in the *now* of his humility and gentleness would be rejected by him in the *not yet* of his glory and power.

The Basis of Final Judgment

Both Jesus' disciples and the church in Antioch misunderstood the nature of Jesus' royal power. Many persons tended to define his royal power as privilege and prestige instead of responsibility and vocation. The dialogue between Jesus and the sons of Zebedee was triggered by their mother's assumption that Jesus would assure her sons positions of personal advantage and authority (20:20-28). The sons shared their mother's misunderstanding as did the ten other disciples. Jesus corrected their mistaken notion of his kingdom. He reminded them that the only way to participate in his royal power was to drink the cup that he was about to drink. His cup was nothing less than the giving of himself in obedience to his calling from God. His disciples would be distinguished not by the power to lord it over others nor by the authority to coerce others. They would be distinguished by the greatness of their service and the exaltation of their slavery. This was true of all Jesus' disciples because their vocation was the same as his vocation: "not to be served but to serve, and to give his life a ransom for many" (20:28).

> In the Final Judgment all that really mattered was how one practiced mercy.

The scene of the Last Judgment in Matthew 25 sets forth the theme of Jesus' royal power. The important words are *his glory* and *the throne of his glory*. Jesus' authority to judge was derived from his glory as the obedient servant of God. Just as he did not minister in his earthly life on his own power, so now he did not judge in his heavenly life on his own authority. The throne on which he sat was his cross, his giving of himself because he had set his mind not on human things but on divine things. The words that summarized what it meant for him to value divine things more than human things were *mercy* and *compassion*. God called Jesus and gathered his followers in order to reveal God's mercy in word and deed. By this means all the nations would receive mercy and practice mercy. Since God desired mercy and Jesus embodied mercy, all the nations would be judged by the standard of his mercy.

Mercy was not something that was done in order to gain something else. It was its own reward because there was nothing greater that could be obtained. The vivid picture of the Son of man coming in his glory and taking his seat on the throne of his glory declared that the ministry of Jesus was the ultimate power and authority of the universe. Belief in Jesus as the Son of man was not a matter of saying the right words about him but rather of choosing mercy as the highest possible good. Belief in Jesus as the Son of man meant action for the sake of those in need: the hungry, the thirsty, the stranger, the naked, the sick, and the prisoner. In the Final Judgment all that really mattered was how one practiced mercy, for "not everyone who says to me, 'Lord, Lord,' will enter the kingdom of heaven, but only the one who does the will of my Father in heaven" (7:21).

The Surprise of Final Judgment

The three parables that Jesus told his disciples just before his teaching about the Last Judgment all contain an element of surprise. The parable about the faithful and the unfaithful slaves makes the point that the master will come on an unexpected day and at an unknown hour (24:45-51). The parade of the ten bridesmaids emphasizes that neither the day nor the hour of the coming of the bridegroom is known (25:1-13). The parable of the talents teaches that on the day of reckoning those who seek to save themselves because of fear of their master will lose their lives (25:14-30). Each parable underscores the fact that no one will escape the surprise of the Last Judgment.

Jesus' teaching about the Last Judgment in 25:31-46 contained the same element of surprise. The separation of people as a shepherd separates the sheep from the goats will be an unexpected experience, because it will be based upon what they have done without their knowing that they have done it. The sheep will be surprised when they hear they are blessed because they gave food, drink, hospitality, clothing, compassion, and sympathy to the Son of man when he was in need. They will ask, "When did we minister to your need?" And he will say, "Just as you did it to one of the least of these who are members of my family, you did it to me" (40).

> One cannot avoid the surprise of the Judgment by looking for the Son of man in advance among the hungry, the thirsty, the stranger, the naked, the sick, and the prisoner.

Likewise, the goats will be surprised when they hear that they are accursed because they did not give food, drink, hospitality, clothing, compassion, and sympathy to the Son of man when he was in need. They will ask, "When did we fail to minister to your need?" And he will say, "Just as you did not do it to one of the least of these, you did not do it to me" (45).

The text affirms that the Son of man is present among the people of the nations in "the least of these." Readers of Matthew are prepared for this identification of Jesus with the little children, the little ones, the poor, the outcast, the sick, and the afflicted (8:14-17; 9:10-13; 10:40-42; 12:1-5; 15:29-31; 19:13-15; 21:14-17).

The new teaching that startles the readers of Matthew is that one cannot avoid the surprise of the Judgment by looking for the Son of man in advance among the hungry, the thirsty, the stranger, the naked, the sick, and the prisoner.

The Son of man is there in "the least of these," but he is always there as a hidden presence. No amount of looking for him will take away the surprise of his presence. Those who spend their time seeking to identify him so that they can escape the mystery of his presence will be surprised to discover that they have missed him. Those who spend their time ministering to the needs of the least of these so that they may practice mercy will be surprised to discover that they have already found their Lord and Master.

This parable teaches about motives for practicing mercy. The desire to flee from the wrath to come, to avoid the surprise of the Final Judgment, is not a fitting motive for practicing mercy. In fact, if one practices mercy in order to save one's life, the result is that one loses one's life. In that case, the center of one's life is still one's self: no matter how one seems to be serving others, one is actually serving self. The ultimate surprise of seeking to save one's life is the loss of one's life.

> The only fitting motive for practicing mercy is to do what is right regardless of the consequences.

The only fitting motive for practicing mercy is to do what is right regardless of the consequences. In fact, if one loses one's life in order to practice mercy, the result is that one finds one's life. In this case the center of one's life is located in the welfare of others: whatever one does is actually serving others. The ultimate surprise of losing one's life in the practice of mercy is to find one's life.

The Result of Final Judgment

The Last Judgment will be a separation of "people one from another as a shepherd separates the sheep from the goats, and he will put the sheep at his right hand and the goats at the left" (32). The basis of the separation is the same for all people, whether or not they have practiced mercy. The surprise of the separation is the same for all: the discovery that what they have done or not done to the least of these is what they have done or not done to the Son of man. But the result of the separation differs for the sheep and for the goats. The sheep are the blessed who will inherit the Kingdom prepared for them from the foundation of the world. The goats are the accursed who will depart from the Son of man into the eternal fire prepared for the Devil and his angels.

The fate of the sheep is that they get what they want. They are those people who in the presence of the needs of others have practiced mercy because they wanted to be merciful. Their reward is to receive that which they have given. "Blessed are the merciful, for they will receive mercy" (5:7). They have valued their relationship with the little ones more than their possessions. They have chosen to be with them in a community of mutual responsibility and cooperation. Their blessedness consists of being with their brothers and sisters in the family of their Lord and Master, the glorified Son of man. Since they have chosen to live in a community of mercy, their reward is reconciliation with themselves, their neighbors, their Master, and their God.

The fate of the goats is that they, too, get what they want. They are those people who in the presence of the need of others have not practiced mercy because they wanted to keep their possessions. Their reward is to be denied that which they have not given to others. Accursed are the unmerciful, for they will not receive mercy (12:23-35). They have valued their possessions more than they have valued their relationship with the little ones. They have chosen to be separated from them in a society of special privilege and competition. Their damnation consists of being separated from their brothers and sisters in the isolation of their own self-centeredness, the glorification of themselves. Since they have chosen to live in a society of self-indulgence, their reward is alienation from themselves, their neighbors, and their God.

Dimension 3: What Does the Bible Mean to Us?

Although the text seems to be a description of the *not yet* of the coming of the Son of man in glory, it is focused clearly upon the *now* of the presence of the Son of man in the hungry, the thirsty, the stranger, the naked, the sick, and the prisoner.

The *not yet* is really none of our business. We neither know the day nor the hour of his coming.

What we do know is that the Son of man is present *now* in the least of these persons. Our business, our vocation, is to serve them *now*. If we serve them *now*, the *not yet* of his coming in glory will be a blessing. But if we do not serve them *now*, the *not yet* of his coming in glory will be a curse.

The Basis of Final Judgment

Mercy matters. Certain things given primary emphasis in the church are not ultimately important. We will not be judged by the Son of man when he comes in his glory on how we have said the right things about him. We will not be judged by the Son of man when he comes in his glory on how we have conducted our public services of worship. We will not be judged by the Son of man when he comes in his glory on how we have understood Scripture. These things may be important, but they are not ultimately important. All of these things must be evaluated by the standard of mercy. If they make us more merciful, then they are useful. But if they do not make us more merciful, then they should either be reformed or discontinued.

What should we do now to prepare for the Final Judgment? The answer is clear: feed the hungry, give drink to the thirsty, welcome the stranger, clothe the naked, care for the sick, and visit the prisoner. Our responsibility is not to make judgments about the least of these but to respond to their needs. Furthermore, our response to their needs is not a matter of convenience but compassion. Now is the time to prepare for the coming of the Son of man in glory by denying self, taking up the cross, and following him.

I have a friend who reminds me every time I see him of what is ultimately important. For more than twenty-five years he has worked to reform the penal system of our state. He is now retired and recently suffered a severe illness. He may never fully recover. But he has not allowed his physical impairment to hinder his ministry to the prisoners. At great personal expense and at some risk to his health, he has continued to advocate prison reform.

When I think about practicing mercy, I see my friend and hear his voice speaking out for justice. I see his actions on behalf of those who are often despised and rejected by society. His life helps me to see that *now* is the time for mercy and that deeds of mercy prepare us for the *not yet* of the coming of the Son of man in his glory.

> Now is the time for mercy. Deeds of mercy prepare us for the *not yet* of the coming of the Son of man in his glory.

The Surprise of Final Judgment

This parable surprises us with the teaching that the *not yet* of the Last Judgment is already here. The Son of man who will come in glory at the end is present *now* in the hungry, the thirsty, the stranger, the naked, the sick, and the prisoner. We will surely miss him if we waste our time looking for him. He is hidden among us and will remain hidden until the end of time. So the parable teaches us to stop looking for him. Instead we are called to minister to the least of these who are always present and visible.

As I reflect on the surprise of the Final Judgment, one person who comes to mind is my high school English teacher. She spent her entire life teaching in a small, poorly equipped, underfunded school. Most of the books in the library came from her own collection. She loved her subject but she loved her students even more. She was both patient and demanding. She would be surprised and embarrassed to read what I have written about her. But I think the ultimate surprise of her life will be to discover that the mercy she gave to the least of these, her students, was the mercy she gave to the Son of man.

The Result of Final Judgment

The judgment of the Son of man when he comes in glory is final. It confirms what has already been done. The separation of the sheep from the goats does not introduce anything new. It simply reveals what has already been established by the choices people have made. We define ourselves as sheep or goats daily as we either give or withhold mercy. In this sense the *not yet* of Final Judgment has already come upon us in the service we render or fail to render to the least of these *now*.

The blessing of the sheep when the Son of man comes in his glory is that they continue to live in the community they have already chosen.

If we have valued the least of these more than our possessions, our reward is the blessing of being with them forever. The curse of the goats when the Son of man comes in his glory is that they continue to live in the isolation they have already chosen. If we have valued our possessions more than the least of these, our reward is the curse of living without them forever.

I felt sad as I witnessed the last years of an elderly woman. She was quite affluent and had no material wants. She was unusually healthy. She chose to live a private and self-sufficient life. She made no effort to be neighborly and let it be known that she neither wanted nor needed anything from her neighbors. She contributed nothing to the various community drives conducted to relieve suffering and to enhance the common good. People in the community knew her attitude. Gradually the people who were soliciting funds for various charities stopped calling on her.

She received what she seemed to value most highly. People left her alone to live her life as she pleased without interruptions. When she finally was confined to a nursing home to live out her last days, no one intruded on her privacy. The last judgment of her life was simply that what she wanted with all her heart was what she received.

Dimension 4:
A Daily Bible Journey Plan

Day 1: Matthew 24:9-14

Day 2: Matthew 24:15-28

Day 3: Matthew 24:29-35

Day 4: Matthew 24:36-51

Day 5: Matthew 25:1-13

Day 6: Matthew 25:14-30

Day 7: Matthew 25:31-46

Matthew 26:30-46

12

THE MINISTRY OF JESUS THE MESSIAH COMPLETED: AGONY AND TRIUMPH

27th Apr.

Matthew 26:1 begins a long passage telling the Passion story of Jesus. This session will focus specifically on Matthew 26:30-35 and 26:36-46.

What to Watch For

- Jesus warned his disciples that all will desert him (26:31).
- Peter declared that though others deserted Jesus he would not. Jesus responded by warning Peter that he would deny him three times that very night before the cock crowed (26:33-34).
- Jesus went to Gethsemane to pray, taking Peter, James, and John to stay awake with him in his grief and agitation (26:36-37).
- He went beyond them and prayed for the cup to pass from him but asked not for what he wanted but for what God wanted (26:39).
- He returned to Peter, James, and John and found them sleeping; he urged them to watch and pray so that they would endure in the time of trial. This happened three times (26:40-45).

> You may want to read the entire Passion story found in chapters 26 and 27 of Matthew's Gospel.

In this session you will experience the failure of the disciples because of their self-confidence and the triumph of Jesus because of his confidence in God.

Dimension 1:
What Does the Bible Say?

1. Was there any difference between the behavior of the other disciples and that of Peter? *No*

2. Why was Jesus grieved and agitated? *disciples weren't staying awake Knew he was to die*

3. Why did Peter, James, and John sleep while Jesus prayed? *Tired. They Thought They had everything in control*

4. For what did Jesus pray? *Thy will be done*

Dimension 2:
What Does the Bible Mean?

The celebration of the Passover by Jesus and his disciples preceded the happenings covered in this session's passages. The betrayal by Judas, the arrest of Jesus, and the desertion of all the disciples (26:17-29; 47-56) follows the happenings in this passage.

Jesus had gathered his new family with him to celebrate the deliverance of Israel from Egyptian bondage; he also had gathered them to give himself for them so that they would be delivered from the bondage of trusting in themselves. Since his disciples did not enter with him into his Passion, they did not enter into his triumph. They asserted their own will, depended on their own strength, and failed to endure in their time of trial.

Divine Things or Human Things

Jesus chose divine things instead of human things (4:1-11; 16:21-28). What happened to him in Galilee, on the way to Jerusalem, and in Jerusalem resulted from his choice. The scribes, Pharisees, and chief priests opposed him and the crowds; and his disciples misunderstood him because he conformed to the will of God. He did not conform to the expectations of humans. The failure of his friends to want divine things more than they wanted human things blurred the division between friends and foes.

His acceptance of God's will for his life exposed Jesus to hatred and death plots. Jesus did not want to suffer and die. However, he wanted to do God's will. He wanted to do it so much that he was willing to die for it. He gave up everything, even his own will, in order to fulfill all righteousness. He did not freely choose to suffer and die. He freely chose God and was willing to accept whatever resulted from that choice.

Setting divine things as the supreme value of his life separated Jesus from both friends and enemies. He felt supremely confident that God was in charge and that his life was secure with God, no matter what might happen to him or his followers. God powerfully and authoritatively overruled rejection, suffering, and death, transforming them into forgiveness, rejoicing, and resurrection. Jesus grounded his confidence in the future in God's action, not his own. His knowledge of God sustained him in his hour of trial.

By contrast, Peter had such confidence in *himself* that he made *no* reference to God or to God's action. Peter saw *himself* as the major actor in the unfolding drama. He trusted *himself* to meet the challenge of the hour. He knew what he would do: "Though all become deserters because of you, I will never desert you" (33). The emphasis upon what he would do blinded him to any perception of God's action and to any awareness of his own limitations. Peter arrogantly believed he was in charge and that he could meet the testing of the hour of trial.

Jesus knew Peter well enough to know that Peter's faith *in himself* would result in failure to stand firm. Peter would not be able to save himself. Peter revealed himself as one whose efforts to save himself resulted in total failure. "Truly I tell you, this very night, before the cock crows, you will deny me three times" (34).

Peter's self-confidence made it impossible for him to receive power from beyond himself. He thought Jesus was questioning his courage, so he affirmed his willingness to die rather than deny him. Peter could not understand that not even the bravest person could do what he was challenged to do. Jesus invited him to discover the miracle of dying to live. Instead Peter affirmed himself and clung desperately to his own will and his own power. His final words to Jesus revealed that he still thought he was in charge and able to save himself: "Even though I must die with you, I will not deny you" (26:35).

> The more Peter trusted in his own power, the more he was cut off from the only power that could keep him faithful in the hour of trial.

Peter represented all disciples in this dialogue. "And so said all the disciples" (26:35). Jesus made a choice about the center of his life; Peter made a different choice about the center of his life. Jesus's choice conformed to the will of God and trusted in God's goodness. Peter's choice conformed to his own will and trusted in his own power. Instead of choosing to follow Jesus, the disciples chose to follow Peter. *Since they had chosen to follow the example of Peter, they would all become deserters because of Jesus (26:31, 56).*

The Failure of Self-Confidence

Jesus asked the inner circle of his disciples—Peter, James, and John—to stay awake with him during his time of deep grief and agitation. As he had identified with them and entered with them into their needs and aspirations, so he invited them now to identify with him in his hour of trial. Very soon now, Jesus would be among them as a little child, powerless, the least of these. They would have an opportunity to receive him and to minister to him by giving themselves for him. Hence he asked them to stay awake with him so that they would be able to serve him as he had served them.

> Jesus had prepared them for this moment by his parables about the necessity of being ready for the coming Day of Judgment. He had specifically taught about the importance of keeping alert and watchful (24:36–25:30).

The disciples were neither indifferent nor callous in the presence of Jesus' need. They simply misjudged their own strength. They still operated out of the assumption that they could save themselves. Jesus had taught that only God could give them entrance into the kingdom of heaven. They clung tenaciously, however, to belief in human control and achievement (18:1-5; 19:13-30). When Jesus warned them about trusting in themselves, they all spoke with one voice to affirm confidence in their own abilities.

Therefore, the disciples slept through Jesus' hour of deep grief and agitation. They missed the opportunity to be merciful to Jesus. They centered their attention on the courage to face an external enemy instead of on the faith to overcome an internal enemy. They had courage. Faith, however, was something God alone could create. Mercy was possible for them only as they died to themselves and lived to God. They knew they had courage. They could fight to the end, living by their own strength and dying on their own terms. They knew that when the hour came to take the sword and die by the sword, their courage would not fail them. But when the enemy appeared, armed with swords and clubs, they resorted to violence. Jesus renounced their violence and refused to accept their help, because they had already gone over to the other side. They resembled Jesus' enemies more than they resembled him. The choice that they made when they slept through his ordeal resulted in the fulfillment of the Scripture: "Then all the disciples deserted him and fled" (26:56).

> The disciples were neither indifferent nor callous in the presence of Jesus' need. They simply misjudged their own strength.

The Triumph of Confidence in God

Matthew confronts the reader with the awesome power of God revealed in the one who seemed to have no power. The biblical text does not declare that Jesus was powerless in his hour of deep grief and agitation. Rather he renounced his own power and became the agent of the only real power, the power of God. From the point of view of the worldly understanding of power expressed by enemies and disciples alike, he seemed stripped of all power. In reality he was filled with the power of God. Everything revealed the action of God in his life—from the dramatic action in Gethsemane to his last word to his disciples after his resurrection in Galilee. Human beings only seemed to be in control as they arrested, mocked, and killed Jesus. God was really in control as God sustained Jesus, used Jesus' mockers to proclaim the gospel, and brought life out of death. Jesus differed from his enemies and his followers in that while they denied the power of God in their actions, he affirmed it.

Jesus had not received the power of God as a gift to possess but as equipment for his vocation. Therefore his struggle in Gethsemane was necessary. His choice to live in conformity to God's will alone made his vocation (saving his people from the sin of trusting themselves) possible. The decisive moments of his ministry up to this moment had been the temptations and the encounter with Peter at Caesarea Philippi (4:1-11; 16:13-28). In those prior experiences of testing he prevailed over external enemies—Satan and the embodiment of Satan in Peter—by setting his mind on divine things rather than human things.

The terrible words he spoke to his disciples about not coming to bring peace on earth were now fulfilled by the sword in his own soul. Would he choose to obey his own will and live under his own authority? Or would he obey God's will and live under God's authority? Everything hung in the balance. If he did not take up his cross and follow God's will, he would not be worthy to be God's Son. If he found his life, he would lose it; but if he lost his life for the sake of God, he would find it (10:34-39).

> The disciples failed totally at Gethsemane; but Jesus triumphed totally.

The disciples failed totally at Gethsemane; but Jesus triumphed totally.

The way in which the disciples fell asleep on the watch *three times* underscored their faith in themselves. Instead of watching and praying, focusing their attention on Jesus and his needs, they slept, giving in to their own needs. The repetition of Jesus' action underscored the way in which he placed his faith in God. Instead of sleeping, Jesus watched and prayed. But note that his confidence in God did not result in Jesus receiving what he wanted. God did not act to spare Jesus from the ordeal of death. Jesus anticipated that he would soon suffer and die. That was his destiny. Nonetheless, he chose what God wanted as the supreme value of

> "The cup" to which Jesus referred in Matthew 20:22 and 26:39 meant one's destiny, as in Psalm 11:6 and Psalm 16:5.

his life. The drama of Crucifixion and Resurrection had not yet unfolded, but his watching and praying in Gethsemane had already resulted in his agony and triumph. When he prayed, "My Father, if it is possible, let this cup pass from me; yet not what I want but what you want" (Matthew 26:39), he had died to himself and had been raised up to victory over death.

Jesus was already leading the way for the disciples. He would go before them to open the way to pass through death to life. The entire record of Jesus' arrest, trial, condemnation, crucifixion, and resurrection climaxed his life of service, revealing that by losing his life he found it. *The cross and the empty tomb did not come unexpectedly at the end of his life but rather were the consequences of his vocation.* "The Son of Man came not to be served but to serve, and to give his life a ransom for many" (Matthew 20:28).

Dimension 3: What Does the Bible Mean to Us?

Matthew 26:30-46 is about the authority and power of God. We choose either to triumph by relying on that authority and power, or we fail by relying on our own authority and power. Jesus' agony and triumph at Gethsemane provide the model for us to follow if we want to be his faithful followers today. The failure of Peter and the other disciples warns us that our own self-confidence leads inevitably to the denial and desertion of Jesus. The confidence of Jesus in the authority and power of God helps us to experience anew the self-giving love of God. God's love goes before us and offers us the possibility of victory over death itself.

Divine Things or Human Things

Power preoccupies us. We see evidence all around us. Since the evidence is so pervasive and so convincing, we assume our power has no limits. We choose to trust human objects more than divine objects without considering the consequences. We believe that we will be able to do whatever is demanded of us on the basis of our own authority and our own power.

> Jesus' dialogue with Peter warns us that trust in ourselves leads inevitably to denial and desertion.

Jesus' dialogue with Peter warns us that trust in ourselves leads inevitably to denial and desertion. The more we protest that "*I* will never desert" and "*I* will die rather than deny," the more we shut ourselves off from the only power that can enable us to stand firm in the hour of trial. Jesus reveals to us that the only genuine authority and power is the self-giving love of God. In spite of all evidences to the contrary, we are not able to control what happens. If we follow the example of Peter, we shall fail. But if we are led by the text to enter into Jesus' agony and triumph, we will discover that dying to self, we live to God.

I gain new insight into the meaning of this Scripture every time I am forced by circumstances to give up my own agenda and control. A few weeks ago our five-year-old grandson came to visit us. I had looked forward to his coming and planned what we would do together. Then he came. Suddenly I was confronted with the fact that my agenda and plans prevented me from enjoying his presence. I found myself compelled to pay attention to him, to conform to his expectations, and to receive more from him than I could give. The result was that we had a marvelous time together.

The Failure of Self-Confidence

One way to study this Scripture is to reflect on it in light of our own tragic experiences of seeking to save our lives. The imagery of the text is powerful: "I will strike the shepherd and the sheep of the flock will be scattered" (Matthew 26:31, quoted from Zechariah 13:7). The more we trust in our own power, the more certain it is that we will be scattered, stripped of our self-confidence, and made to become what we really are, God's little ones.

> Evil powers do not inflict the cross on us; the cross happens because of the goodness of God.

Several years ago I was in the midst of what I thought would be a rewarding climax to my professional career. I had planned wisely, achieved my goals, and earned what I expected to receive. Then I was scattered in ways that led to a radical transformation in my life. It was not what I wanted nor was it what I felt that I deserved. In many ways I was stripped of my own authority and my own power. I became aware of my limitations and my inadequacies. But as I look back on it now, I can say honestly that it was the best thing that could have happened to me. I think I have learned to understand more clearly what Jesus meant when he said, "Truly I tell you, unless you change and become like children, you will never enter the kingdom of heaven. Whoever becomes humble like this child is the greatest in the kingdom of heaven" (18:3-4).

The Triumph of Confidence in God

Jesus' triumph in Gethsemane foreshadowed his death and resurrection. However that triumph was not something he accomplished on his own but something God accomplished in him. We need to keep this observation clearly in mind so that we will not assume that confidence in God is something we can attain on our own.

The picture of Jesus watching and praying in Gethsemane shows us someone who absolutely depended upon God. Jesus received real power when he renounced his own power. If we use the text to strengthen our own self-confidence, we misuse it and find it leading us to failure rather than to triumph. *Our hope is grounded not in our resolve to watch and pray but in the fact that when we sleep through the crisis, God in Christ comes to us and offers us again the love that never fails.* And wherever we go, his risen presence awaits us to save us from ourselves.

Several months ago a young man called to ask me for help in paying his rent so that he would not become homeless. I made an appointment to see him. I appraised his need and was able to get the money required for his rent. I became more involved with him as he talked about his past and future.

One thing he needed was a job. He told me that he needed someone to work with him on a maintenance project that would pay him enough for his next month's rent. I agreed to help him and brought my tools to work with him. Obviously, he was not able to cope with his situation without my help. What was not so obvious was the fact that I needed him. I entered into the relationship aware of my own authority and power and committed to doing all that I could for him. As I grew in the relationship, I discovered the limits of my own authority and power and became open to receiving what he could do for me. This strange and disturbing experience left me pondering how the risen Christ comes to us in the "least of these" and offers us the possibility of entering with him into the kingdom of heaven.

Dimension 4:
A Daily Bible Journey Plan

Day 1: Matthew 26:1-5
Day 2: Matthew 26:6-16
Day 3: Matthew 26:17-25
Day 4: Matthew 26:26-35
Day 5: Matthew 26:36-46
Day 6: Matthew 26:47-56
Day 7: Matthew 26:57-75

Matthew 28:1-20

13

THE MINISTRY OF JESUS THE MESSIAH CONTINUED: COMMISSION AND PROMISE

The story of the resurrection of Jesus (Matthew 28:1-20), like the story of his birth (1:18-25), emphasizes that God is the major actor.

PARALLELS IN MATTHEW'S STORIES OF JESUS' BIRTH AND RESURRECTION

Angel revealed God's action in the conception and birth of Jesus to Joseph (1:20-23)	Angel revealed God's action in the resurrection of Jesus to Mary Magdalene and the other Mary (28:1-8)
Obedience of Joseph completed God's action at Jesus' birth (1:24-25)	Obedience of Mary Magdalene and the other Mary complete God's action at Jesus' resurrection (28:7-8)
Role of Tamar, Rahab, Ruth, Bathsheba, and Mary in accomplishing God's creation of a people (1:1-18)	Role of Mary Magdalene and the other Mary in accomplishing God's salvation of a people (27:55-56; 28:1-10)

This session focuses on Matthew 28:1-20, which you will want to read. It also draws on many of the texts we have considered already in our study of the Gospel of Matthew.

What to Watch For

- Mary Magdalene and the other Mary went to Jesus' tomb as the first day of the week was dawning (28:1).
- A great earthquake interrupted the visit to the tomb. An angel of the Lord came and rolled back the stone and told the women not to be afraid; announced that Jesus the crucified had been raised; showed the place where he lay; and ordered them to go and tell the disciples that Jesus had been raised and was going ahead of them to Galilee where they would see him. The women obeyed with fear and great joy (28:2-8).
- Jesus met them and said, "Greetings!" They seized his feet and worshiped him. Jesus repeated the order that the angel gave them (28:9-10).
- When the guards reported everything to the chief priests, the chief priests bribed them to report that Jesus' disciples had stolen his body (28:11-15).
- The disciples obeyed the instruction of the women and gathered on the appointed mountain in Galilee. There they saw and worshiped Jesus, though some doubted (28:16-17).
- Jesus had been given all authority in heaven and on earth; he ordered them to make disciples of all nations by baptizing them in the name of the Father and of the Son and of the Holy Spirit, and teaching them to obey his commands. Jesus further promised to be with them to the end of the age (28:18-20).

In this session you will experience anew the resurrection of Jesus as the end of the old age of violence and death and the beginning of the new age of mercy and life.

Dimension 1: What Does the Bible Say?

1. What did the earthquake and the rolling back of the stone from the tomb by an angel of the Lord signify?

2. Why did the women leave the tomb with fear and great joy?

3. Why did the chief priests bribe the guards to lie about what had happened at the tomb?

4. Why did Jesus order his disciples to make disciples of all nations by baptizing them and teaching them to obey his commandments?

5. Why did Jesus promise his disciples that he would be with them to the end of the age?

Dimension 2: What Does the Bible Mean?

Some disciples in the church at Antioch accepted the tradition about Jesus' resurrection without internalizing it or applying it to their lives. Although they might have affirmed that Jesus had been raised from the dead, they lived as if it had not occurred. The profession of their lips was denied by the practice of their lives.

Matthew sought to help his readers understand the resurrection of Jesus as the end of the old age and the beginning of the new age. He wanted them to recognize the denial of the resurrection of Jesus as a futile attempt to cling to the security of the old age, and to affirm the resurrection of Jesus as their calling to continue his ministry to the end of the age.

Entering the New Age

Matthew 28 begins with a grim reminder that God's good gift of a day of rest for all creation had been so misused and perverted that it had been transformed into a day of death. God gave the sabbath laws so that God's people would live in dependence upon God and accept God's gifts. Instead those sabbath laws had become rigid rules for excluding others and claiming special privileges for those in power (12:1-14). The resurrection of Jesus occurred "after the sabbath, as the first day of the week was dawning" (1). The text suggests that something more important than the passing of time had taken place. The old order had come to an end; a new order was beginning.

The new beginning started at the place where the old order seemed to be most secure: the tomb. Jesus had been executed as a common criminal, condemned by the religious and political authorities, taunted by bandits executed with him, mocked by his executioners, and derided by those who

> The new beginning started at the place where the old order seemed to be most secure: the tomb.

passed by. Soldiers guarded his tomb. A stone secured and sealed it. Mary Magdalene and the òther Mary came to the tomb to see the dread symbol of Jesus' defeat by his foes and his desertion by his friends.

God's intervention transformed their desperate mission. An angel of the Lord descended from heaven, rolled back the stone, and sat upon it. The tomb was not only open; it was completely defeated. Suddenly an earthquake struck, symbolizing that God's time had come (24:3-8). The opening of the tomb was God's work. The angel was God's agent. But until the angel spoke to the women, no one knew what had happened. The supernatural event left the guards terrified and lifeless. Human comprehension failed. The dawning of the new age depended upon the revealing word spoken by the angel and heard by the women.

Angel - A spiritual being serving God and supporting humanity. Angels are God's messengers of encouragement to believers. They appeared at the birth of Jesus, after his temptation, and at the Resurrection.

The women continued to be afraid when they heard the word of the angel. But their fear changed in form from terror of the unknown into reverence for the mystery of God's presence. The angel spoke about the Jesus they had known and followed, and—yes—watched from a distance as he died. But his death was not the end; it was the beginning. God raised up the crucified so that the world would know God's invincible power, everlasting authority, and self-giving love.

The women had claimed no status among Jesus' followers. They had been lost in the nameless crowd of women who served him, from whom came the unknown anointer at Bethany. These women had not deserted him. Now they were singled out and named. Mary Magdalene and the other Mary entered the new age first and carried first the good news to the eleven who had deserted him.

The women set out on their journey to tell the deserters of their Lord that he had not deserted them. In fact, he waited for them to gather again in Galilee. The women obeyed the word of the angel. The angel's message transformed their journey to the tomb into their mission to the scattered sheep. As the Lord's messengers, the women continued to serve him, as they had by following him and providing for him in Galilee. And as they journeyed they discovered that he was with them. He greeted them and blessed them, calling them to be his ministers to his brothers. So they left the tomb—the old age of violence and death—and went quickly to obey the word of the angel. Blessed by Jesus' presence, they worshiped him and proceeded to tell the disciples of the new age of mercy and life.

Clinging to the Old Age

Matthew's Passion narrative consistently pictures Jesus' enemies as pathetic. They seized Jesus and condemned him to death, but God was in charge.

They mocked Jesus, but God used their mocking to proclaim the good news. They sought to seal his tomb with a stone and make it secure with a guard of soldiers, but God opened the tomb and transformed it into a symbol of triumph. All of their efforts to remove Jesus from the scene and to contradict his life and teaching failed. They discovered they had no power to seal him in the tomb nor to secure the tomb as a sign of their victory over him. They only succeeded at revealing by their words and actions that they were powerless in the presence of the invincible power and everlasting authority of God in Jesus who was crucified and had been raised from the dead.

Jesus' enemies included more than the chief priests, elders, scribes, Pilate, the crowds, and the Roman soldiers. They represented all persons who valued the security and privileges of the old age more than the opportunity and challenges of the new age. They trusted violence and death more than they trusted mercy and life. They interpreted the Scriptures to exclude others and to protect their possessions rather than to include others and to use their possessions to serve them. Matthew invited his readers to recognize in his description of Jesus' enemies those attitudes and actions keeping people from entering into the joy of the new age. These texts were never intended to justify hatred of the Jews nor to shift blame onto the Romans. Matthew wanted to call readers of his Gospel to repentance.

Living as if the Resurrection never occurred expressed more than anything else the clinging to the old age in the presence of the new. The soldiers at the tomb supported this delusion when they sought security from the chief priests. The guards reported what had happened as if the authorities in Jerusalem were still in charge. The chief priests assembled the whole council to plan what to do as if their decision would settle the matter. They bribed the soldiers to tell a lie and promised to protect them from the governor, acting as if a lie were more powerful than truth. They pretended that one who could kill the body was more to be feared than one who could destroy both soul and body in hell. They lived as if the Resurrection had not occurred, trusting themselves more than God, using their power and their possessions to protect themselves, and misusing their money to corrupt those whom they were called to lead.

Serving the New Age

The new age dawned for the scattered disciples when they submitted to the truth brought to them by the women. They no longer cowered under the lie of the old age. Jesus called them back to their origin, to Galilee, to the mount where Jesus taught them, and to the mount of his transfiguration. There they gathered once again. Jesus restored them to his community by the power of the same love that had led them to begin their journey with him. They recognized in his risen presence the one whom they had met by the sea, followed through villages and towns to Jerusalem, and deserted in his hour of trial. They were still the same little ones, and he was still their stricken shepherd; yet now they saw him as the one whose love was the invincible power and everlasting authority of God. They worshiped him as the dearest treasure of their hearts, though they continued to be frail and weak ("some doubted"). Nonetheless, Jesus blessed them and called them to his service. Once they had been scattered by the incredible mystery of his love. Now they were gathered by the invincible power and everlasting authority of his love. The little children had come home to their Lord and Master.

The new age dawned for the scattered disciples when they submitted to the truth brought to them by the women rather than cowering under the lie of the old age.

Jesus now held authority to command their obedience because he had emptied himself of his own authority and become the agent of God's authority. This authority was not the authority to lord it over others nor to coerce others; it was the authority to serve and give his life as a ransom for many. Jesus' resurrection was the mighty act of God, clearly designating his self-giving death as the ultimate power and the everlasting authority of the universe. Jesus claimed for his work by his power and authority those who experienced his resurrection.

The eleven, gathered on the mountain in Galilee, represented the reconstituted and reformed people of God. They were now commissioned to do for the nations exactly what Jesus had done for them. Jesus saved them from themselves by making them his disciples. Now they were sent to do for others what had been done for them. The resurrection of Jesus fulfilled God's promised salvation. The vocation that Jesus had entrusted to them signified that they had been saved by the Resurrection. The salvation they were now to offer to the nations would become confirmed as the nations became disciples and accepted their vocation to practice mercy.

The idea of baptizing the nations probably startled Matthew's readers. So far as we can tell, Jesus never baptized anyone. But now baptism "in the name of the Father and of the Son and of the Holy Spirit" was the first thing the disciples were ordered to do in order to make disciples of the nations. Rather than serving as an imitation of something Jesus did for others, baptism includes others in the baptism Jesus himself experienced. The authority and power of God that surrounded and empowered Jesus at the beginning of his own ministry would make the nations into disciples.

It was impossible for humans to save themselves or to save others. God's power revealed in Jesus and available through the Holy Spirit was the source of all salvation. The vocation of the disciples to make more disciples of the nations was a human impossibility. But for those who accepted their vocation from God, to make disciples of the nations was possible, for with "God all things are possible" (19:26).

The source of salvation was God; but salvation awaited fulfillment in the lives of obedient disciples. Therefore, salvation that began with baptism in the name of the Father and of the Son and of the Holy Spirit was completed by "teaching them to obey everything that I have commanded you" (20). The vocation to make disciples was carried out in the nurture of the faithful community.

Jesus taught not about rules and regulations but about mercy. Since the eleven had learned what mercy meant by receiving mercy, they were qualified to teach mercy to the nations. They needed to remember that Jesus would always be with them as they practiced mercy.

Baptism was the sign of God's mercy. Jesus' commandments were the content of mercy. But the real presence of mercy was in the mysterious identification of the risen Lord with the least of these: the hungry, the thirsty, the stranger, the naked, the sick, and the prisoner. To the extent that disciples practiced mercy to the least of these, Jesus' presence with them would be a blessing. To the extent they failed to practice mercy to the least of these, Jesus' presence with them would be a curse. The one who commissioned the disciples to continue his ministry by going to the nations would come again in glory to judge all the nations.

> **Baptism** - Rite of initiation into the Christian community. It probably arose from the Jewish practice of baptizing Gentile converts to Judaism when they were circumcised. It was first mentioned in connection with John the Baptist and was associated with the confession of sins. Jesus was baptized by John to "fulfill all righteousness." Jesus did not baptize during his earthly ministry, but after his resurrection he commanded his disciples to baptize "in the name of the Father and of the Son and of the Holy Spirit."

Dimension 3: What Does the Bible Mean to Us?

Although most of us have accepted the traditions about the resurrection of Jesus, we have often lived as if the Resurrection had not occurred. Perhaps the reasons for this fact arise from our failure to ask what difference the resurrection of Jesus makes in the way we live. Matthew's witness helps us to ask this question and to reflect on it in light of our own faith journey.

Entering the New Age

The resurrection of Jesus means that the old age of violence and death has come to an end. The new age of mercy and life has begun. The last word about Jesus is not the tomb sealed and guarded by his enemies but the stone rolled back by God and interpreted by the angel of the Lord.

> We also experience great joy to discover that when we leave the tomb of the past, we enter into the promise of the future.

The Resurrection confronts us with a choice concerning who is in charge and who exercises real power and authentic authority. Those who choose to trust in the victory of God over death reveal their choice by becoming servants of life, by going to others with the word of life, and by announcing that the risen Lord will be seen by all who hear and obey the word of life.

In the words of the resurrection angel, God speaks to us. We experience fear when we are told that all the old securities and assumptions have been shattered and replaced by the new age of God's triumphant love. The risen Lord blesses us with his presence and confirms us in his service. The promise that others will see him is one that we make with confidence because we have been greeted by him and encouraged by him on the way.

Those persons, who are gentle and humble in heart, who like Mary Magdalene, the other Mary, and the many unnamed women—those who have followed Jesus and provided for him—lead the way into the new age of the Resurrection. One such woman retired recently after years of faithful service as director of an inner-city settlement house. She has seen the tomb of shattered hopes and ruined lives, but she has also heard the word of the angel. She has left the tomb with a word of hope for her scattered brothers and sisters. Often she has feared the mystery of God's promises, yet she has also known the joy of being greeted by the risen Lord and seeing his presence in her work.

I asked her what she would do in her retirement. She replied that she did not know exactly what she would do, but she was sure that an opportunity for service would open before her. She based her confidence upon the fact that the risen Lord has always met her and confirmed her in her work.

Clinging to the Old Age

Matthew's text does not justify our condemnation of others for their failure to enter the new age inaugurated by Jesus' resurrection. We read it properly when we allow it to focus our attention upon our own attitudes and actions that hinder entrance into the new age. Perhaps we often cling to the old age because we think that our security depends on the status quo and the authorities who exercise worldly power and authority.

One of the corrupting lies of the old age is that violence and death prevail over mercy and life. We subscribe to this lie when we support war as a means of promoting our individual and national security. The plain teaching of the crucified and risen Lord is that "all who take the sword will perish by the sword." Yet we persist in believing that violence and death will result in life. This lie is still told and believed among us to this day. We shall not enter the new age of mercy and life until we repent of our clinging to the old age of violence and death.

A few years ago our home was robbed while we were attending the Christmas Eve service in our church. Obviously the thieves had watched our home so that they could break in and steal our treasures while we were away. When we returned and discovered that the thieves had taken many things of little monetary value to them but priceless to us, we felt outrage.

I personally felt overcome with a sense of irreparable loss and righteous indignation. My immediate reaction was to wish that I could do violence to those who had done violence to me. As I reflect on that painful experience in light of my study of this text, I am compelled to think of what happened not so much in terms of the evil done to me but rather in terms of my response to that evil. I know now that as long as I harbored violent thoughts and contemplated vengeful action, I still clung to the old age of violence and death.

Serving the New Age

The resurrected Lord gathers us into his community so that our special relationship to him will be shown in the world as our special responsibility to continue his ministry of mercy. Since the gift of his mercy makes us his brothers and sisters, we are commissioned to make disciples of all the nations by practicing his mercy. We do not worship him perfectly; doubt often cripples us. But Jesus keeps coming to us in his risen power, revealing that he has all authority in heaven and on earth by loving us enough to entrust his work to us.

> The resurrection of Jesus is not an idea to debate but a vocation to accept.

We know that what has happened to us is a human impossibility. Jesus makes us his disciples through the power of the Father and of the Son and of the Holy Spirit. Therefore we know that he can use us to make disciples of the nations because the Father and the Son and the Holy Spirit work within us. We go in obedience to his calling because, wherever we go, he is already there in the least of these, his brothers and sisters. Everything that is necessary has already been accomplished. He is always with us, to the end of the age. But *how* he will be with us is dependent upon us.

One of my life's turning points occurred when I was in college. I was trying to decide my life's work, my vocation. One night I attended a revival meeting in one of the local churches. I found the sermon especially relevant for me.

After the service I arranged to have a conversation with the preacher. I don't remember anything that he said in his sermon, and I can't recall now what we discussed in our conversation. I do remember, however, that he was gentle and humble in heart. He did not try to coerce or manipulate my response. He listened intently, encouraged me to speak openly and honestly, and affirmed my dignity and worth. My life was changed by his ministry because he was filled with the power of the Father and of the Son and of the Holy Spirit. He surrounded me with mercy and taught me mercy simply by showing mercy. My brief encounter with him has helped me to understand what the risen Lord said to the eleven disciples on the mountain in Galilee: "And remember, I am with you always, to the end of the age" (28:20).

Dimension 4:
A Daily Bible Journey Plan

Day 1: Matthew 27:1-14
Day 2: Matthew 27:15-31
Day 3: Matthew 27:32-54
Day 4: Matthew 27:55-66
Day 5: Matthew 28:1-10
Day 6: Matthew 28:11-15
Day 7: Matthew 28:16-20

GLOSSARY

Antioch- [an'tee-ok] A city in Syria about twelve miles east of the Mediterranean Sea. The Gospel of Matthew may have originated in Antioch about A.D. 85.

Bethany- [beth'uh-nee] A village on the east slope of the Mount of Olives, two miles east of Jerusalem. Jesus lodged here during the Passover week.

Caesarea Philippi- [ses'uh-ree'uh-fil-ip'*i*] A city on the southern slope of Mt. Hermon. Peter confessed Jesus as "the Messiah, the Son of the living God" in the region of Caesarea Philippi.

Capernaum- [kuh-puhr'nay-uhm] A city on the northern shore of the Sea of Galilee. Jesus made his home there after he moved from his ancestral village, Nazareth.

Centurion- [sen-tyoor'ee-uhn] The commander of a "century"—one hundred soldiers—the smallest unit of the Roman army.

Cross- An instrument of torture and execution, its use probably originated among the Persians and was adapted by the Romans as a punishment for slaves, for non-citizens, and occasionally for citizens guilty of treason.

Cup- Symbolizing the pleasant or bitter experiences of life, Jesus used it symbolically to refer to his passion.

Decapolis- A confederation of ten Hellenistic cities settled in Palestine after the death of Alexander the Great (323 B.C.). They included a mixed population and were distinctly anti-Jewish.

Demon- A spirit with minor powers. The New Testament depicts demons as evil spirits exercising malevolent influences.

Galilee- The northernmost region of ancient Israel, it was a region of Jews and Gentiles. Most of Jesus' ministry took place in Galilee.

Gentiles- [jen'til] A non-Hebrew (non-Israelite) person.

Gethsemane- [geth-sem'uh-nee] The place where Jesus went to pray during the night on which he was betrayed.

Hades- [hay'deez] The realm of the dead, derived from the name of the Greek god of the underworld. During the New Testament period, it was regarded as a place where the deceased awaited judgment.

Harvest- The gathering of agricultural crops. Passover marked the barley harvest in April or May; Pentecost occurred during the wheat harvest in June; and Booths or Tabernacles celebrated the grape harvest in October. Jesus referred to the harvest symbolically as the task of enlisting followers for the kingdom of God and also as the consummation of God's promises at the end of the age.

Jerusalem- [ji-*roo*'suh'luhm] The city of David, holy city of Judaism, Christianity, and Islam. Many of the events of Jesus' last days took place in or near Jerusalem.

Jordan- [jor'duhn] The largest and most important river in Palestine, extending over two hundred miles from its sources near Mt. Hermon in the north to its outlet in the Dead Sea. During part of his public ministry Jesus traveled along the eastern bank of the river, and he crossed it at Jericho as he began his final journey to Jerusalem.

Judea- [*joo*-dee'uh] The Greek and Latin form of Judah. During New Testament times Judea was used loosely to refer to nearly all of Palestine.

King- A male ruler with supreme authority. After the destruction of the Davidic monarchy, an idealized king became the hope for the restoration of Israel. Such a king would be the Messiah, the descendant of David, and the savior of the people. The importance of this idealized king increased as the political situation in Israel worsened.

Kingdom of heaven- (kingdom of God) That realm ruled by God. In Hebrew thought it gradually came to signify not a geographical area or a political entity but an allegiance of faithful individuals.

Leprosy- A broad generic term for any number of eruptive skin diseases and disorders. Lepers were considered ritually unclean and the laws regulated contact with them.

Messiah- [Christ) Literally "anointed one"; "Messiah" from the Hebrew, "Christ" from the Greek. *Messiah* refers specifically to Jesus' vocation to "save his people from their sins." His anointment was actually his calling by God to his ministry of preaching, teaching, and healing.

Naphtali- [naf'tuh'l*i*] Land in northern Palestine, especially vulnerable to foreign invaders, it is described as the region of darkness and gloom that received the light of salvation in Jesus' public ministry (compare Zebulon).

Nazareth- [naz'uh-rith] A city in Galilee where Jesus grew up. Mary and Joseph settled there when they returned from Egypt. Jesus moved from Nazareth to Capernaum at the beginning of his public ministry. He returned at least once to his boyhood home, where his message was rejected.

Palestine- [pal'uh'st*i*n] A geographical designation for the region inhabited by the people of Israel. Strategically located at the southwestern end of the Fertile Crescent, it forms a land bridge connecting Asia Minor and Mesopotamia with North Africa. In ancient times it was traversed by important commercial and military roads.

Pharisees- A movement within Judaism of the late Second Temple period (150 B.C.–A.D. 70). The Pharisees were noted most for their strict observance of the Jewish religion, their accurate exposition of the law, their handing down of extra-biblical customs and traditions, their moderate position with regard to the interplay of fate and free will, and their belief in the coming resurrection and in angels.

Priest- A mediator between God and humankind, who instructed the people in God's laws concerning conduct and worship. The priest officiated in the offering of sacrifices. After the destruction of the Davidic monarchy, the priestly hierarchy in Jerusalem took over the political as well as the religious leadership of the people. Neither Jesus nor his disciples rejected the legitimacy of the priesthood and sacrifices.

Sabbath- The seventh day of the week, observed as a day of rest in Israelite and Jewish religion since earliest times. The controversies in which Jesus was involved with regard to the sabbath all hinged on his authority as a teacher over against the Pharisees' interpretations of sabbath laws or on the legality of redemptive acts normally forbidden as work on the sabbath.

Sadducees- [sad'*joo*-sees] A sect existing within Judaism from some time in the second century B.C. to A.D. 70. They were the party of those with political power. They accepted only the written Torah and rejected all oral interpretation or tradition. They rejected the doctrine of the future resurrection, belief in angels and spirits, and views of the Pharisees. Their influence among the common people was quite limited.

Samaritans- Inhabitants of the region of Samaria and adherents of the Samaritan religious tradition. Samaritans came to be regarded as neither fully Gentile nor fully Jewish. *Samaritan* could itself be a term of contempt among Jews. The Samaritan's Scripture contained only the Pentateuch. They regarded Moses as the final prophet of God and a superhuman being. Samaritans appear in positive roles in Jesus' teaching and the record of his ministry.

Sanhedrin- [san-hee'druhn] A council in Jerusalem that functioned as the central judicial authority for Jews. Ideally the Sanhedrin included seventy members plus the high priest who served as the president. It was composed of representatives of the leading priestly families and the religious instructors known as "scribes." Also included were "elders" who were not connected with the scribes or priests.

Scribes- Interpreters and teachers of the Mosaic law. The scribes came to be addressed with respectful titles, particularly "Rabbi" ("my master, my teacher"). At the root of the conflict between Jesus and the scribes lay the question of his independent interpretation of the Scriptures (Torah).

Sea of Galilee- The larger of the two lakes in northern Palestine, located in the region in which Jesus conducted most of his public ministry. The lake is thirteen miles long and eight miles wide at its widest point. It is where Jesus called his first disciples. He crossed and recrossed it frequently during his ministry.

Shepherd- A common occupation in ancient Palestine, often used metaphorically in biblical narratives. Because shepherds were the sole source of provision and protection for sheep in the ancient Near East, *shepherd* came to be applied to God, who guides and cares for the people. Jesus is called a shepherd as the leader and guard of his people, as the one who suffers for his people, and as the final judge of the nations.

Sin- The failure of human beings to live the life intended for them by God, their creator. Sin in its basic sense is always ultimately against God rather than against humankind. The fundamental effect of sin is alienation between God and the person or society that sins. Reconciliation is the heart of what is accomplished in God's salvation of humankind. God initiates the process of reconciliation, but a human response to God's action is always required.

Son of David- A title used to affirm that the Messiah is a descendant of King David. Jesus' royal lineage is the result of divine intervention instead of mere human procreation.

Son of God- One who shares a close relationship to God. In the Hebrew Scriptures a "son of God" was one who had a divine commission for a specific task. Obedience to the task was often contained within the concept. Except in the Gospel of John, Jesus die not call himself "Son of God." God addressed Jesus as "Son" in the Gospel of Matthew.

Son of Man- Jesus' favorite self-designation in Matthew, Mark, and Luke. It is used by Jesus to describe his ministry and authority on earth, to predict his suffering and death, and to refer to his coming as the judge of the nations at the end of the age.

Synagogue- [sin'uh-gog] Buildings used for Jewish worship and instruction in the Scriptures. They came into being during the Persian period (539-330 B.C.). In time the synagogues came to be the focal point of Judaism. After the destruction of the Temple in A.D. 70, the synagogue made possible the survival of Judaism. The synagogues were the center of the Jewish community in any town with a Jewish population and were used for political functions, including judgment of Jewish violators of the Jewish law.

Syria- [sihr'ee-uh] In ancient times, the region bordering the eastern Mediterranean and extending northward from (and sometimes including) Palestine and Phoenicia to the Euphrates in the northeast and the Taurus mountains of southern Turkey in the northwest. Its capital was Damascus and one of its principal cities, Antioch.

Tax collector- A person employed by a wealthy entrepreneur who purchased the rights to a tax franchise. The ordinary tax collector sat in a tax office and collected taxes, or sat by the roadside and inspected the goods of those who were traveling and charged a toll tax. Because the tax collectors were Jews working for the hated Romans, they were considered traitors by fellow Jews. They were well known for their greed because after paying their employer, they were free to keep the surplus for themselves. They were despised by the Pharisees.

Temple- Solomon built the first Temple in Jerusalem between 958 and 954 B.C. The Babylonians burned it to the ground in 587/586 B.C. Efforts to rebuild it began in 537 B.C. and it was restored in 520 B.C. In 20-19 B.C. Herod dismantled it and began to replace it with one of grander design constructed in Hellenistic-Roman style. It was destroyed by the Romans in A.D. 70 and never rebuilt.

Zebulon- [zeb'yuh-luhn] The territory of Zebulon is used symbolically in Matthew to affirm that the ministry of Jesus includes "those who sat in the region and shadow of death."

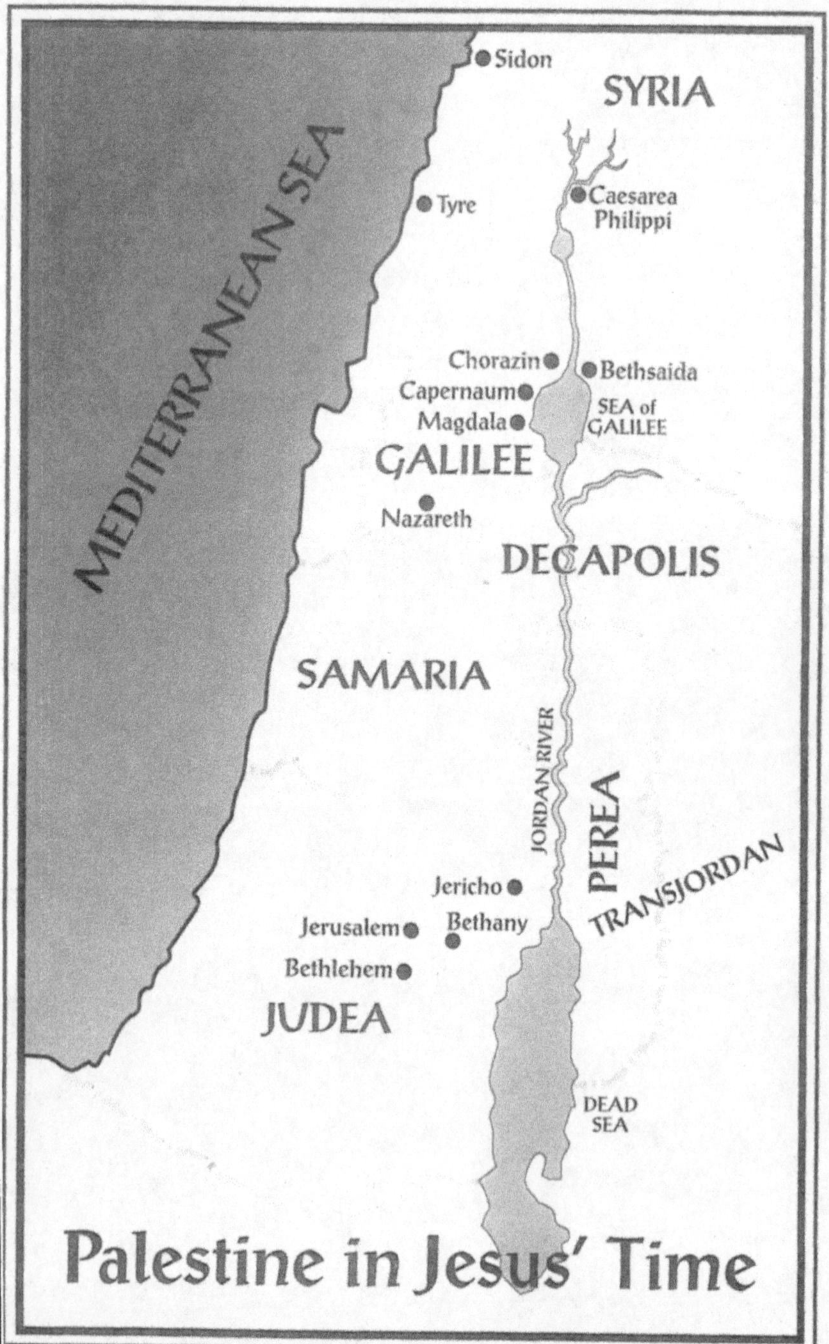

Palestine in Jesus' Time